How to Design
Bead & Wire
Jewellery

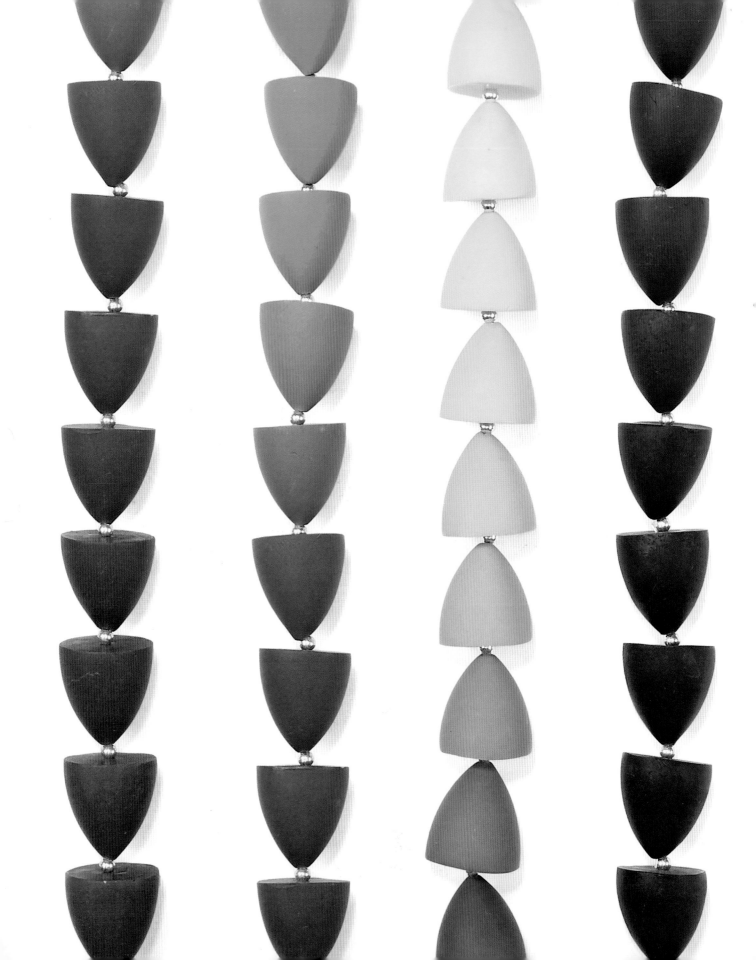

How to Design Bead & Wire Jewellery

Everything the
beginner jeweller
needs to know

Renata Graham

Search Press

A QUARTO BOOK

Published in 2011 by
Search Press Ltd
Wellwood
North Farm Road
Tunbridge Wells
Kent TN2 3DR

ISBN: 978-1-84448-689-2

Conceived, designed and produced by
Quarto Publishing plc
The Old Brewery
6 Blundell Street
London N7 9BH

QUAR: DBEA

Senior editor: Lindsay Kaubi
Text editor: Liz Jones
Additional text: Kate Pullen
Art editor and designer: Jacqueline Palmer
Design assistant: Kate Bramley
Photographer: Simon Pask
Illustrator: Coral Mula
Art director: Caroline Guest

Creative director: Moira Clinch
Publisher: Paul Carslake

Colour separation by PICA Digital Pte Ltd, Singapore
Printed in Singapore by Star Standard

10 9 8 7 6 5 4 3 2 1

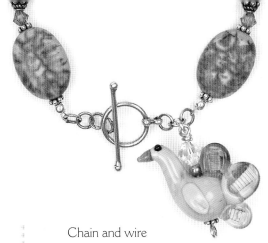

Contents

Author's foreword

I am a professional jewellery maker and I have taught jewellery-making classes to beginners for 20 years, teaching them how to design and make their own beaded jewellery. During this time I've learned a lot about bead and wire jewellery design and I've put this experience into this book.

I have tried many different types of art and craft activities over the years, but I've always returned to beads and wire because there are so many different design possibilities. This can be a problem though for beginners, who often struggle to get started – overwhelmed by the many possibilities, or concerned that their ideas won't work.

Should you sketch or lay out your designs? Which colours go together? What beads are available? Where can you find inspiration? What should you avoid doing? Which types of beads or wire can you combine? What other materials are there, and what designs suit different types of people or occasions?

This book aims to guide you through the process of answering those questions for yourself, and is unique as it first teaches you these design skills so that you never feel lost or struggle to get started. It then shows you the tools, techniques and project ideas that you can use to bring your designs to life.

Renata Graham

About this book

This book is organized into four chapters, guiding you through the design process from finding inspiration to choosing materials and essential techniques.

CHAPTER ONE: DESIGN ESSENTIALS (PAGES 8–35)

This chapter takes you through the design process in detail, from colour theory and finding inspiration to sketching, bead texture and finishes and all the practical considerations of designing bead and wire jewellery.

CHAPTER TWO: SIMPLY BEADS (PAGES 36–69)

Organized by material this comprehensive directory of beads advises on the advantages, disadvantages, ideal stringing materials, key properties and design options for all the bead types shown.

CHAPTER THREE: OTHER MATERIALS (PAGES 70–83)

Using the right findings, wire, spacers, clasps and joiners is essential for a professional finish to your jewellery designs. This chapter guides you through all of the options available and helps you to make a good choice.

CHAPTER FOUR: TECHNIQUES AND ESSENTIAL PROJECTS (PAGES 84–135)

The inspiring projects in this chapter take you through a broad range of techniques used to make bead and wire jewellery. Starting with simple stringing, the projects become progressively more challenging, including wire shapes and chains and multiple-strand bead stringing.

Chapter one: Design essentials

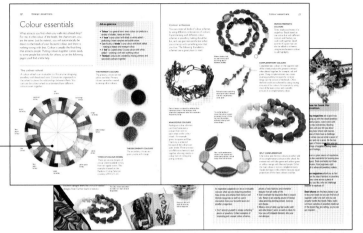

Design is discussed in detail, starting with colour theory.

There are lots of tips and techniques for finding inspiration.

Chapter two: Simply beads

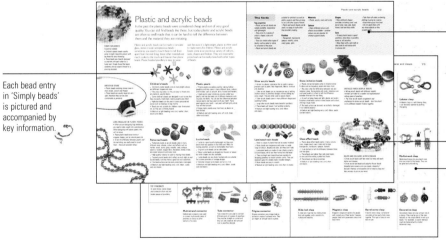

Each bead entry in 'Simply beads' is pictured and accompanied by key information.

The key facts about each type of bead is summarized at-a-glance for each category.

Examples of jewellery made using the bead type illustrate each bead category.

Comprehensive listings of 'other materials' provide information on where, when and how to use stringing materials and findings.

Chapter three: Other materials

Chapter four: Techniques and essential projects

All the tools and materials needed are clearly listed.

Handy notes on beads appear through the chapter.

Making up techniques are laid out with step photographs and clear instructions.

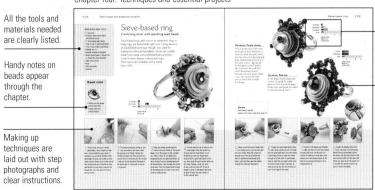

Variations on the main design illustrate how small changes can reinvent a piece of jewellery.

Proportion of colours used

Proportion and type of metallic beads used

Pieces are accompanied by a graphic device that identifies the proportion of metallic and coloured beads in each piece.

Design essentials

Colour is usually the first thing that attracts people and every colour can produce a variety of shades and tones. In this chapter you are going to learn about colour theory and how and why different colour combinations work. You will also learn about practical design considerations: where to find inspiration; bead textures and finishes; accent colours, patterns and repeats; jewellery design styles for hair, head and body, and the range of necklace lengths commonly used.

Colour essentials

What attracts you first when you walk into a bead shop? For me, it's the colour of the beads; the chances are, you are the same. Just by instinct, you will automatically be drawn to the beads of your favourite colour, and there is nothing wrong with that. Colour is usually the first thing that attracts people. Putting colours together comes easily to some people but is tricky for others, so on the following pages you'll find a little help.

At-a-glance

- **'Colour'** is a general term: every colour can produce a variety of shades, tones and tints.
- A **'tone'** is any colour with black or white added – producing a more complex and subtle colour.
- Specifically, a **'shade'** is any colour with black added – making a deeper and stronger colour.
- A **'tint'** (or **'pastel colour'**) is any colour with white added – creating a soft and soothing colour.
- **'Tertiary'** colours are created by mixing primary and secondary colours together.

The colour wheel

A colour wheel is an invaluable tool for anyone designing jewellery with beads and wire. Colours are organized on the wheel to show the relationships between them. You can use the colour wheel to understand how different colours work together.

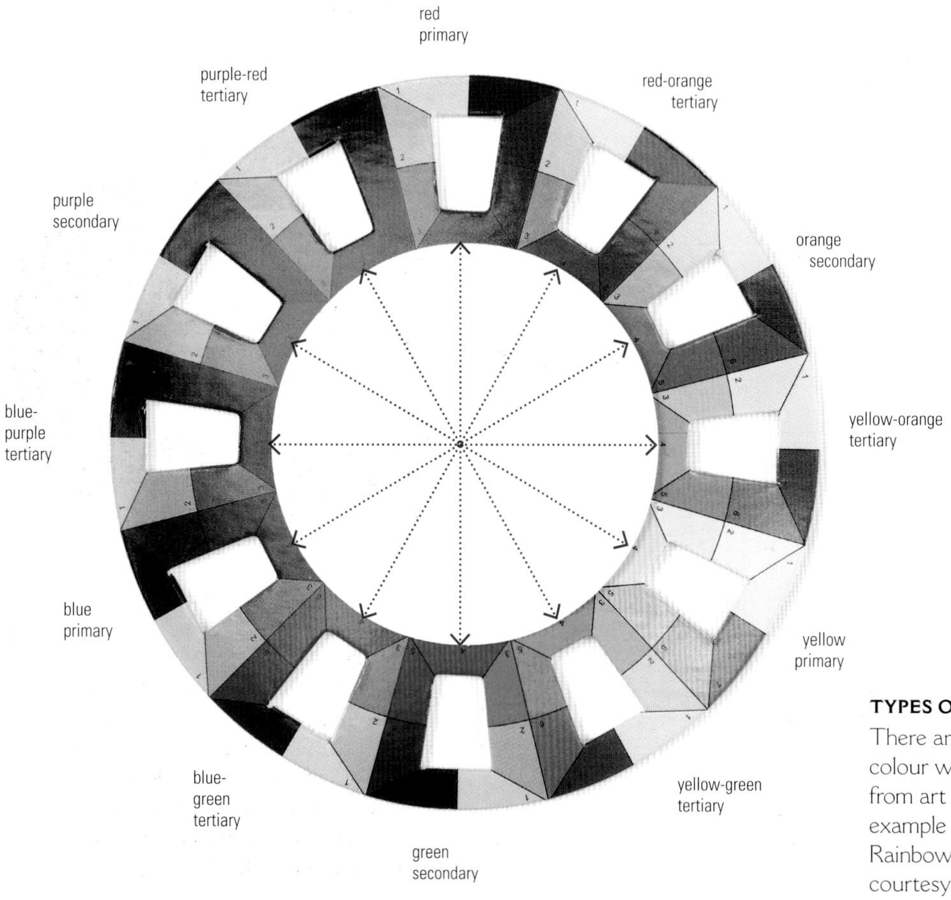

red
primary

purple-red
tertiary

red-orange
tertiary

purple
secondary

orange
secondary

blue-
purple
tertiary

yellow-orange
tertiary

blue
primary

yellow
primary

blue-
green
tertiary

yellow-green
tertiary

green
secondary

THE PRIMARY COLOURS
The primary colours are red, yellow and blue. Primary colours cannot be created by mixing other colours.

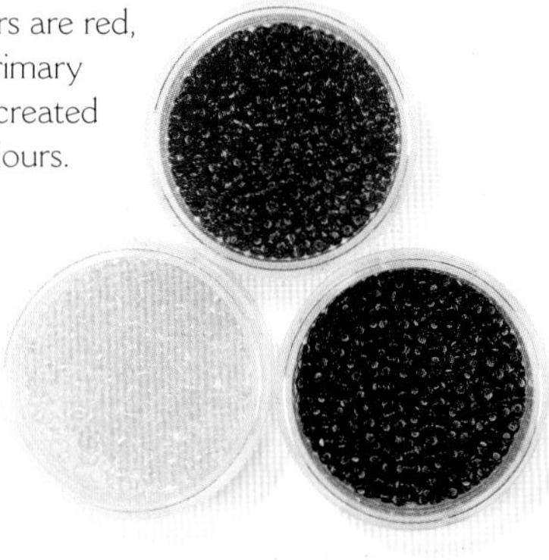

THE SECONDARY COLOURS
The secondary colours are green, purple and orange.

TYPES OF COLOUR WHEEL
There are several designs of colour wheel available to buy from art supply stores. This example is based on the Rainbow Colour Selector, courtesy of KIC2, LLC.

Colour schemes

You can create all kinds of colour schemes by using different combinations of colours. Experimenting with different colour schemes in jewellery making should be fun, and can give real satisfaction when you come up with something new that you love. The following 'foundation schemes' are a great place to start.

Different shades of red are used to make a bold and striking piece of statement jewellery.

MONOCHROMATIC COLOURS

Tints, shades and tones of a single hue. Beads based on one colour but with different textures and finishes can work well together. Small accents of a pure hue can also be added to schemes using monochromatic colours to add highlights.

COMPLEMENTARY COLOURS

Complementary colours on the opposite side of the wheel produce the greatest contrast when placed together, for example, red and green. Using complementaries can create stunning jewellery, because the contrast brings out the colours of the beads. Often, the best results are achieved by using varying amounts of the colours, for example by using more of the main colour and a smaller amount of a complementary colour.

Plenty of interest is achieved by combining three harmonious colours in this analogous colour scheme that complements rather than overwhelms the jewellery design.

Red beads create eyecatching accent points when combined with their complementary colour, green.

The careful blending of colours from yellow to purple encourages the eye to follow the line of the necklace without introducing harsh colour changes.

ANALOGOUS COLOURS

Analogous colour schemes use three harmonious colours from next to each other on the colour wheel – for example, green, turquoise and blue. Harmony is achieved because all the colours are quite similar. These are easy yet effective schemes to put together, allowing variety in colour but not risking any jarring contrasts.

Here, a split complementary scheme of red, turquoise and yellow-green produces a vibrant design where red dominates.

SPLIT COMPLEMENTARY

One colour plus the two colours on either side of its complementary colour on the wheel, for instance red with blue-green and yellow-green, or yellow-orange with blue and purple. Either the main colour or its two complementaries should dominate in this scheme because equal proportions of the three colours could jar.

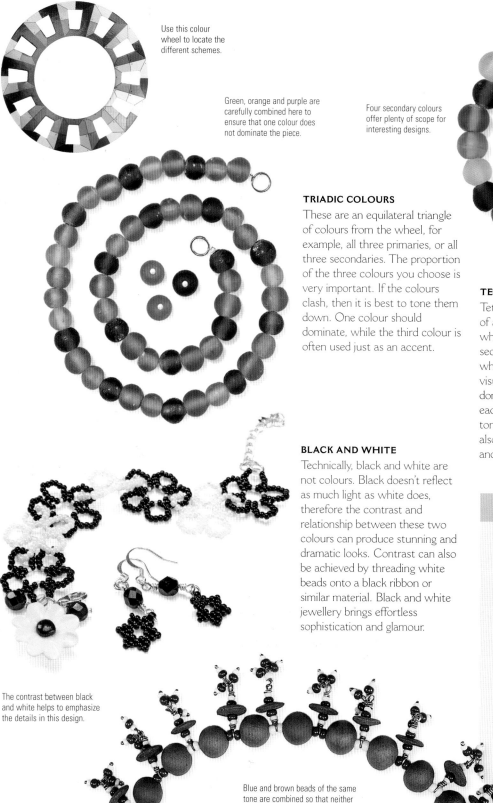

Use this colour wheel to locate the different schemes.

Green, orange and purple are carefully combined here to ensure that one colour does not dominate the piece.

Four secondary colours offer plenty of scope for interesting designs.

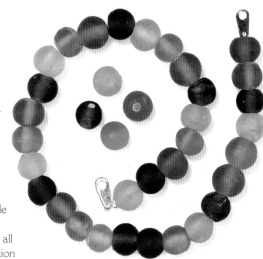

TRIADIC COLOURS

These are an equilateral triangle of colours from the wheel, for example, all three primaries, or all three secondaries. The proportion of the three colours you choose is very important. If the colours clash, then it is best to tone them down. One colour should dominate, while the third colour is often used just as an accent.

TETRADIC COLOURS

Tetradic colours are four colours at the corners of a square or rectangle placed on the colour wheel. This tetradic colour scheme uses secondary colours from around the colour wheel – purple, green and orange. The strong visual contrast also works well if one colour dominates and the other two complement each other. For a better result, keep similar tones together – so if you use a blue-green, also use a blue-purple rather than a pure green and a pure purple.

BLACK AND WHITE

Technically, black and white are not colours. Black doesn't reflect as much light as white does, therefore the contrast and relationship between these two colours can produce stunning and dramatic looks. Contrast can also be achieved by threading white beads onto a black ribbon or similar material. Black and white jewellery brings effortless sophistication and glamour.

Tonal Value

Value refers to whether a colour is naturally light or dark. Lemon yellow has a very light tonal value, appearing almost white, while indigo has the darkest tonal value, appearing almost black. It is sometimes difficult to judge tonal values. The eye looks at the colour first, and doesn't immediately consider the tonal value. One way to comprehend this is to imagine taking a black-and-white photograph of the colours. Which beads would be the palest grey, and which the darkest grey?

The contrast between black and white helps to emphasize the details in this design.

Blue and brown beads of the same tone are combined so that neither colour dominates.

These striking blue beads emphasize the cool nature of this colour scheme.

Rich reds and pinks combine to create a necklace that has a feeling of warmth. The red hearts reinforce this sensation.

TEMPERATURE

Warm colours – reds and oranges – are dominant; cool colours – blues and violets – tend to be recessive. If two colours of equal temperature are placed together they vibrate. The temperature is altered by any background colours. If the background is warm, then the colour appears cooler; and if cool, it appears warmer. Even when using colours lying opposite each other on the colour wheel (a complementary colour scheme) you can still achieve an overall warm feeling as long as you use more of the warm colours, and fewer of the cool ones.

HARMONIOUS COLOURS

Colours that are said to be in 'harmony' sit within any quarter of the wheel. Draw a circle to the same size as the colour wheel, and cut out one quarter. Placing this on top of the wheel, and turning it around, shows the harmonious sections clearly.

Harmonious colours can be used to create jewellery with plenty of interest but which does not feel cluttered with colour.

Bright multicoloured beads turn an otherwise simple design into a head-turning necklace that is fun and easy to wear.

Shades and tints

The intensity of a colour scheme can be decreased by using colour shades or tints. Adding black to a colour gives a shade, so, for instance, dark blue is a shade of blue. Adding white to a colour gives a tint, pale pink is a tint of red and lemon is a tint of yellow. All of the colour schemes can be made from the shades or tints of a colour to make a more muted or neutral piece of jewellery.

Shades and tints of blue showcase the subtle twisted design of this bracelet.

MULTICOLOURED

In this multicoloured piece, which uses the whole colour spectrum, the warm red beads stand out the most, while the cooler blue beads and tints, such as pale pink, recede. Metallic beads recur throughout the piece and bring the scheme together. The tints and shades used help to vary the tone.

Inspiration

Bead jewellery designers have an eclectic mix of
design elements to work with, giving an almost
endless variety of colour and form combinations.
With such an exciting range of design possibilities it
can sometimes be difficult to know where to start,
however inspiration for great jewellery designs is all
around us when you know where to look.

Flowers are a great
source of inspiration for
colour, shape and form.

Colour

Bead jewellery designers work with a
colour palette that covers the entire
spectrum of shades and hues. Keep looking
around you for colour combinations that
work well together or perhaps unusual
colours that are combined with striking
results. Look at how colours are used as
accent points or to create an overall
ambience. Nature is a great source of
inspiration and a trip to a park or garden
can provide a surprising range of ideas.

Inspiration is everywhere. This
neckpiece was inspired by a piece
of driftwood, and even uses
driftwood as one of its parts.

Trends

Jewellery and fashion go hand-in-hand.
Keep an eye on the latest fashions and
draw inspiration from new trends. Look at
how fashion designers team items of
jewellery on the runway or imagine what
jewellery set you would team with popular
trends on the high street. Don't restrict
yourself to contemporary fashions. Some
of the most exciting and innovative designs
call on inspiration from the past, whether
it's retro designs from the 1970s or classic
designs from further back in history.

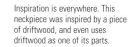

The vivid colours of fruit
salad provide inspiration
for bright colours from
citrus orange through
to berry red.

The colour, texture and pattern
of a fabric can inspire unusual
design ideas.

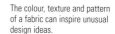

Keep up to date with
trends by browsing
fashion magazines.

Shape and form

Bead jewellery gives you the opportunity to work with an exciting range of shapes. Architecture is a fantastic source of inspiration for both shape and form. A modern skyline with its range of often contradictory designs shows how different shapes combine to produce an overall effect. Shapes are also used as accents and feature points. Collect interesting shaped items in a resource box. Being able to touch and feel a shape will help you to appreciate its form and these are useful as inspiration when you are creating new jewellery designs.

Texture

Richly textured beads can add dramatic interest to your designs. Beads created from fabric or yarn often have a tactile quality that brings a whole new dimension to your designs. Use your sense of touch to feel items and determine what feels comfortable against the skin as well as what looks great. Look at clothing designs as well as items of jewellery to see how textures are used as part of a design.

Jewellery

As a designer you will want to produce your own unique designs. However jewellery from other designers, both contemporary and from the past, can be a great source of inspiration. Look for design elements that you can interpret and how these will translate to your own designs.

Unusual objects – in this case miniature tarot cards – are used to create an eclectic piece of jewellery with an emphasis on shape and texture.

Beads themselves can be a source of inspiration. Visit bead shops and fairs and see what ideas develop.

Beading magazines provide a wealth of inspiration, plus projects and techniques for you to try.

Places to look for inspiration

Beading magazines are a good way of keeping up with the latest jewellery ideas and projects; some come with step-by-step instructions. Beading magazines will also tell you about upcoming bead shows and courses, and some of them have a challenge section where you can enter a piece of jewellery and win a prize. On the last few pages of these magazines you can find listings of suppliers selling beads tools, and findings.

Books are a great source of inspiration and are also wonderful for learning new techniques. There are books out there for everyone, from beginners right through to advanced jewellery makers.

Fashion magazines allow you to find out what the latest fashions in jewellery are. If you come across a piece of jewellery you like, why not challenge yourself to replicate it?

Bead shows are the best places to go to buy your beads as you can find lots of suppliers under one roof and you can actually handle the beads. Many stalls will have samples of jewellery made out of the beads they are selling, so you can get inspired.

Keep an inspiration scrapbook

An inspiration scrapbook can be an invaluable resource when you are designing jewellery. Keep photos and articles from fashion and lifestyle magazines as well as useful information from your favourite bead and jewellery magazines.

- Don't restrict yourself to simply collecting photos of jewellery. Collect examples of interesting and unusual colour schemes,

photos of new fashions and innovative designs from all walks of life.

- Don't overlook the inspiration that is around you. Nature is an amazing source of design ideas providing exciting colours, textures and shapes.
- Make a note of what you feel works well and what doesn't work, as well as ideas for how you will interpret elements into your own designs.

Sketching

Sketching can help you to visualize your project. Don't worry; your drawings don't need to be perfect, as long as you can understand them. Sketching your design is simply about planning the look of your jewellery by drawing it on paper, including the shape of the beads and other necessary components.

Take the sketch with you to the bead shop (a bit like a shopping list) – that way you won't forget to buy any of the beads and components you need for your project. It is also quite useful to keep a small sketchbook and pencil in your bag, in case you come up with ideas while you are away from your workshop.

MAGAZINE CUTTINGS
Tear pictures with interesting jewellery designs out of magazines, and keep them for reference. You could put them in a dedicated folder. Gathering a visual library of styles you like can be useful for future projects; you can adapt them to your personal taste.

A TYPICAL SKETCH
Keep your sketch clear and simple; though you can use coloured pencils to try out different colours. Jot down the names of the materials and components to be used for the project – use short terms: 'pendant', 'cord', 'clasp', 'chain'. If you are drawing the sketch for someone else, you may decide to include more detail.

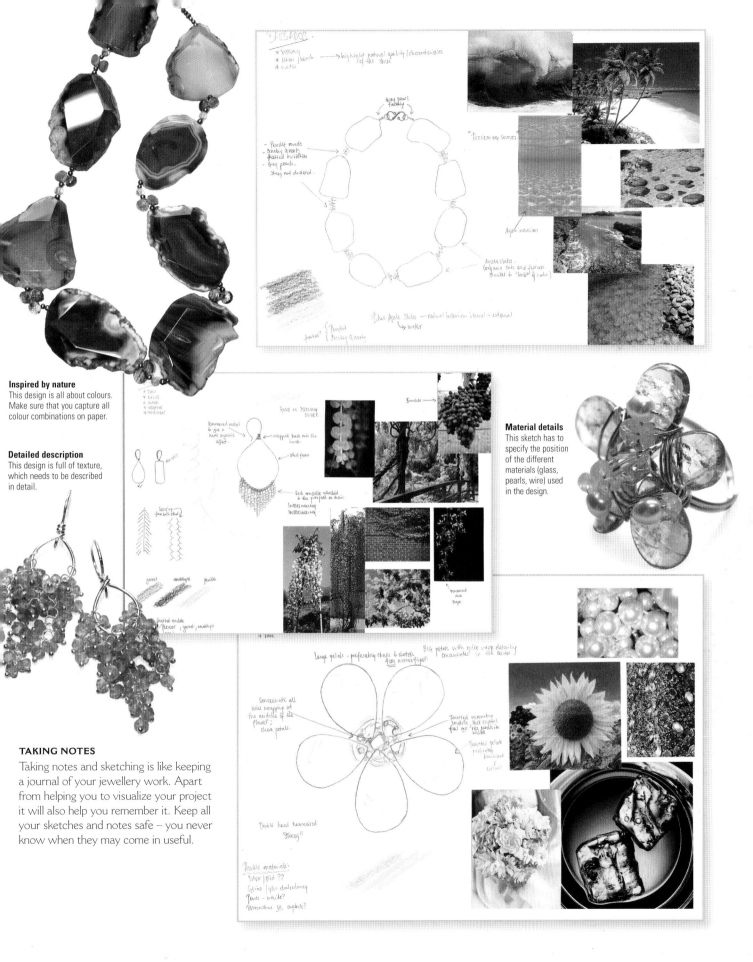

Inspired by nature
This design is all about colours. Make sure that you capture all colour combinations on paper.

Detailed description
This design is full of texture, which needs to be described in detail.

Material details
This sketch has to specify the position of the different materials (glass, pearls, wire) used in the design.

TAKING NOTES

Taking notes and sketching is like keeping a journal of your jewellery work. Apart from helping you to visualize your project it will also help you remember it. Keep all your sketches and notes safe – you never know when they may come in useful.

Initial layouts and maquettes

Laying out your design with your final beads and materials can be fun and allows you to test the look of the finished design. Beading boards and mats can save you a lot of time at this stage.

Beading boards and mats are very easy to use and are readily available from bead shops at reasonable prices. They come in a range of different sizes and colours – think about what would be best for your particular needs.

Beading board

There are many different types of beading boards but most of them will have one or more long grooves or channels around the board, where you lay out your beads, marked with numbers or lines. In the centre or at the sides of the board will be small compartments where you can keep your beads and findings. Some boards also have shorter grooves or channels in the middle for needles. Marked and numbered grooves are especially helpful when designing multiple-strand jewellery as you need to clearly see the different lengths of parts of your design. Once you have placed your beads into the compartments, the fun begins. You can start to play with the beads by arranging them in different combinations and patterns until you are happy with your design – and then you are ready to go ahead with stringing.

Arranging your beads

Once you have organized your beads into the compartments on your bead board, you can start designing. The easiest way is to start with a central bead and then work your way to the ends. Don't be afraid to rearrange your beads until you are completely happy with your design. If you have a beading board with a few channels, you can always make more than one sample (if you have enough beads) and keep them in the channels next to each other to see which one you prefer.

Bead design boards

Planning your design before stringing becomes a lot easier with this specially designed board with its useful grooves and measurement indicators.

Using a bead design board: Bead design boards are creative and practical spaces where you can experiment with the colour, shape, size and length of your beads before you string them all together into a final piece. Here's how it works:

The grooves: The grooves on a design board are for you to place your beads in, and will help you to plan the individual strands of your finished piece. Experiment with colour choices and the order of your beads here. Most bead design boards come with three grooves, which enable you to plan a multistrand piece and see how the different strands will interact.

Measurements: Around the outside and inside edges of the board are measurements to help you work out the exact length of your piece. When laying your beads on the board, make sure you don't leave any gaps as this will give you an inaccurate length.

Containers: A bead design board has useful indentations that will hold beads and findings as you work.

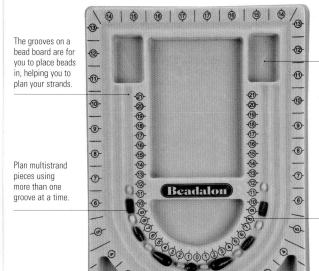

The grooves on a bead board are for you to place beads in, helping you to plan your strands.

Plan multistrand pieces using more than one groove at a time.

Hold beads and findings in the useful indentations to keep everything together.

Use the measurements to work out exact lengths.

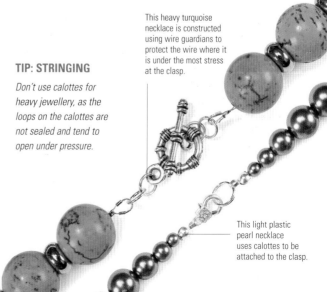

INCLUDE THE CLASP
Don't forget to include the length of the clasp when arranging your beads and, when designing multiple-strand jewellery, remember that the outside strand will be the longest one.

BEADING MATS
Beading mats are washable and you can easily roll them up to transport them, for example if you are going on holiday and you would like to take your project with you.

Visualizing and weight testing

Make a simple strung example to test the layout of your jewellery and its finished weight before you start crimping. Use bead stoppers to keep the beads from falling off the ends of the strand and to maintain the tension of your project – or bulldog clips can do this job. Place the necklace securely onto your own neck or a jewellery bust (around the neck) and let the weight of the beads pull your necklace down. Now you can see how the necklace is going to sit and you can make any necessary adjustments. The weight of beads should keep the necklace centred and balanced. It is better to have an uneven number of beads, especially if you have a definite centre point (a larger bead or pendant, for instance).

Beading mats

Beading mats are made out of material that keeps your beads and findings from rolling away, especially the tiny components like crimps and seed beads. Beading mats come in different sizes and colours. They are also good for laying out your beads and trying them out in different arrangements.

Choosing the right clasp

Once you are happy with your design and the weight of your necklace, it is time to choose the appropriate clasp. This will likely come down to personal choice and preference. However, lightweight necklaces are often finished with calottes, and small- or medium-sized clasps such as spring rings and lobster clasps. Heavyweight necklaces can be finished with more than one crimp and larger types of clasps such as toggles and hooks (see page 74).

Keeping the wire hidden

Larger beads tend to pull on stringing wire, causing the tiny sections of wire between individual beads to be seen. This situation can be avoided by using spacer beads or bead caps or both to break the angle of the wire.

TIP: STRINGING

Don't use calottes for heavy jewellery, as the loops on the calottes are not sealed and tend to open under pressure.

This heavy turquoise necklace is constructed using wire guardians to protect the wire where it is under the most stress at the clasp.

This light plastic pearl necklace uses calottes to be attached to the clasp.

10 design considerations

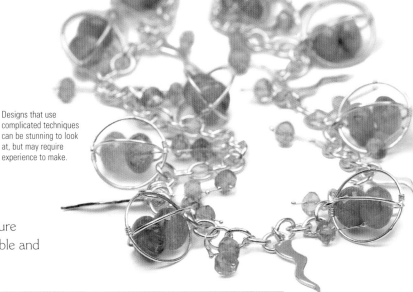

Designs that use complicated techniques can be stunning to look at, but may require experience to make.

Great jewellery design is more than simply creating jewellery that is nice to look at. A number of other considerations need to be taken into account to ensure that your jewellery is attractive to look at, comfortable and safe to wear, practical to make and affordable.

Earring drops work well on both clip-on and pierced earring fittings.

Very long earrings may not be suitable for everyday wear and may be impractical for certain professions; take this into account when designing.

Bright colourful beads on elastic are ideal for children to wear.

1. Beauty is in the eye of the beholder

Consider who is going to be wearing your jewellery when you start the design process. Determine whether there are any special design requirements, such as the lifestyle of the wearer.

One of the keys to successful jewellery design is the ability to translate an idea. A subtle change of colours or shapes of beads in the piece can transform a design, giving you the opportunity to tailor your designs to different people.

2. Comfort

Jewellery should be a pleasure to wear; therefore, ensuring that your designs are comfortable to wear, as well as looking great, should be an important consideration in your design process. Consider features such as the weight of beads or the flexibility of the stringing material.

3. The age of the wearer

When it comes to age considerations, this is often about practicality, such as not making bold, semiprecious stone jewellery for a child and not attaching any fancy clasps to jewellery for older people, as they might have difficulties working them. However, teenagers and younger people can wear almost anything; here you can let your imagination run wild.

4. Practical to make

When you are designing jewellery it is essential that you consider the production process as well as the overall finished effect. Make sure that you are familiar with all the techniques required to make one of your designs. This is particularly important when adding fittings and findings, such as clasps. If you are unfamiliar with a technique or want to try something new, practice first. If necessary 'road test' an item by wearing it for a few days yourself.

5. Affordable

Whether you are creating an item of jewellery as a gift or an item to sell, budgetary implications are an important factor to consider. If the cost of making a piece is going to render it unaffordable then it's time to go back to the drawing board. Happily, there are many ways that you can introduce subtle changes into your designs to reduce costs. Consider, for instance, recycling elements from old pieces of jewellery. This is an exciting way to introduce low cost elements into your designs as well as providing unique feature points.

Reusing beads from secondhand jewellery is a great way to keep costs down.

6. Function and form

One of the challenges that many jewellery designers face is balancing function and form. This means creating a piece of jewellery that combines beauty and practicality. The key to achieving this balance is to determine how the jewellery will be worn and for what purpose at the start of your designing process.

- A piece of jewellery that is for everyday wear should be sturdy and robust. This means that all the materials, including beads, stringing material, and findings, such as clasps, should be of a suitable quality.
- An item of jewellery, however, that is for occasional wear need not be subject to the same considerations. Here you can go to town with creating a stunning item that need not stand up to the rigours of everyday wear.

7. Safety considerations

- **Allergies:** Some people may have an allergic reaction to metal, especially to nickel and cobalt. Look for hypoallergenic alternatives and ensure your supplier conforms with any relevant safety standards.
- **Children's jewellery:** To keep children safe, children's jewellery shouldn't contain any sharp objects or break easily. Elastic stringing material is good to use. Don't give jewellery to children under the age of three to avoid a choking hazard.
- **Magnetic findings:** Magnetic jewellery findings are not suitable for pacemaker wearers or pregnant women.

8. Materials

The materials from which beads are made are numerous, and include semiprecious stones, metals, freshwater pearls, wood, bone, crystal, acrylic and many others (see the examples on page 68). Jewellery materials are loaded with cultural meanings: commitment, desire, luxury, monetary value, etc. Just keep this in mind when designing your project.

9. The wearer's preferences

Is your wearer a man or woman? What is their job? Do they play extreme sports? When will they wear the jewellery? Is it for a special occasion? Consider personality and lifestyle – outgoing or shy? Do they wear big and bold jewellery, or prefer more gentle and subtle designs? What about a modern or vintage look, metal or natural materials, gemstones or crystals, gold or silver, long or short? Will they struggle with the clasp? Would they prefer a necklace, bracelet, earrings or a matching set? These are all questions you should ask yourself.

Lightweight jewellery, such as this coin bead necklace, is perfect for everyday wear.

This striking piece may have a tendency to catch on clothes or other items if used for everyday wear.

Very heavy beads – like this crystal heart pendant – and multistrands are best suited to occasional wear.

10. Skin tone

Skin tones are often divided into seasons: 'winter' (brunettes and dark skin), 'summer' (natural blonds or brunettes with pale skin), 'autumn' (redheads or brunettes with brown eyes) and 'spring' (strawberry-blond hair). Skin tones can also divided into two categories: 'cool' (dark complexions) and 'warm' (reddish complexions). Decide what category your wearer falls into; here are some recommendations for the two types.

Warm skin:
* **Metals** – gold, bronze, copper
* **Stones** – coral and amber
* **Colours** – orange, yellow, green, brown

Cool skin:
* **Metals** – silver, white gold, platinum
* **Stones** – pearls and diamonds
* **Colours** – purple, pink, blue, red

Choosing the right beads for the right person

Do you know who you're making your jewellery for? — **NO** ▶ *Consider using elastic or memory wire as they aren't so size dependent. Or you could use another method but add an extender chain.*

YES ▼

Is it a child or someone who has a problem using a clasp? — **YES** ▶ *Memory wire or elastic are easier for someone who can't use a clasp – or for children's jewellery where you want to ensure the piece will come off or break if caught.*

NO ▼

Do they only wear a certain style of jewellery or have specific tastes? — **YES** ▶ *Make your choice based on what they love. Go with thread and pearls for someone who loves a classic look; or cord and large beads for someone after a bolder look.*

NO ▼

Do the beads you want to use have any obvious characteristics? — **YES** ▶ *If your beads have sharp holes, consider flexible beading wire with crimps or memory wire.*

Metal beads or charms are less likely to damage memory wire.

Large holes may be better with cord or ribbon.

Tiny holes may suit flexible wire or thread.

If the beads lack colour, try jazzing them up with coloured cord or thread.

NO ▼

Are you after a certain look or style? — **YES** ▶ *Floaty and feminine? Try ribbon or yarns with cord ends. Bold and masculine? Maybe dark cord or metal memory wire. Soft and subtle? Go for illusion cord and use few beads. Big and heavy? Cord, memory wire or flexible wire are just right to take the weight and look of heavy beads. Multistrand? Flexible wire with end cones will hide unsightly ends.*

NO ▼

Do you want to specifically hide or show the stringing material? — **YES** ▶ *Flexible wire, cord, thread and memory wire can all be hidden. However, if you want, they can all also be made to play a part in the final design.*

NO ▼

Lastly, are you looking for a quick result or a polished look? ▶ ▶ *All stringing can be quick and easy, but using thread and knots can be more time-consuming. You will find that they give a professional, polished finish.*

Size, shape, balance and weight

Understanding how size, shape, balance and weight work together is at the heart of successful bead jewellery design. These are the design fundamentals that will help you create stunning designs that are comfortable to wear.

Shape

Factor the shape of the beads, as well as the shape of the finished piece, into your designs. The shape of the individual beads will influence the end design and they will also determine the weight and wearability of the finished piece. Lots of small irregular beads, for instance, will create a highly textured effect, however this may be uncomfortable to wear close to the skin. The shape of beads is also important when you are selecting feature beads. Shaped beads are particularly useful when you are making themed jewellery, for instance heart shaped beads are perfect for a gift for a romantic occasion.

Size

The size element of design includes the size of the finished piece as well as the dimensions of the individual beads. Not only are these important features in their own right but the ratio between the two will dramatically alter the appearance of a piece of jewellery. A necklace made from a myriad of tiny beads will look completely different to the same length necklace made from bold feature beads.

Balance

Balance is an essential part of jewellery design. This includes ensuring that the weight of a piece of jewellery is well balanced as well as the finished effect being pleasingly balanced to the eye. Balance does not mean that an item needs to be too structured or formal in the design. Creating striking items of asymmetrical jewellery, for instance, involves considering how balance influences the design. This is particularly important with necklaces that are designed to fall in a certain way. If the weight is balanced incorrectly the necklace may twist. As a result, at times, finding a solution that offers both visual and physical balance can be a matter of compromise.

Weight

The weight of a piece of jewellery will affect how comfortable the jewellery is to wear. This will also influence how a piece of jewellery hangs or sits in place. A very heavy necklace will hang completely differently to a lightweight necklace, creating a very different finished result. Weight is particularly important to factor into designs for earrings as heavy earrings can pull on the lobes. Individual beads will also impact the finished weight of an item and by altering the size or material of the beads you may be able to change the weight of the finished item.

Asymmetrical designs require careful planning to ensure that the end result is attractive and not the result of a stringing mistake.

Irregular shapes help to create visual interest.

Fit tips

Creating a piece of jewellery that is the correct size for the wearer is crucial if the jewellery is to look good and be worn often. If you know the person you are making the jewellery for then you can take their measurements and factor this into your design. If you don't know the measurements, for instance if the jewellery is for a surprise gift or to sell, then you may need to consider the supplies you are using:

- Flexible stringing material, including elastic and memory wire, will give you some flexibility in your designs and can be stretched a little to fit if required. This is particularly useful with bracelets.
- Use an extension chain (a small chain that extends the length of a necklace). This is a useful way to make a necklace larger.
- Adjustable findings, such as split shank rings, are designed so that the size can be adjusted. This can be a good way to make jewellery that will fit a variety of sizes.

An extension chain will make a bracelet or necklace larger and with careful planning will become an integral part of the design.

Supplies

The size, shape, balance and weight of your jewellery designs will influence the findings and stringing supplies that you use.

- **Shape:** pick findings that complement the shape of your design. This includes selecting a clasp that reflects the shape of the beads and using coordinating spacer beads.
- **Size:** the size of the beads will affect the size of stringing material that you use. Very small beads are likely to have tiny holes that will require thin wire or beading thread.
- **Balance:** select stringing material that will cope with the weight of your finished design and also provide the flexibility you require.
- **Strength:** choose a clasp that will be strong enough to hold the weight of the finished piece. On the other hand, if you have a light necklace and a heavy clasp, the clasp will pull the necklace forwards and down – and the wire may cut unpleasantly into the skin.
- **Weight:** check that your beading thread or wire is strong enough for your design. Many beading thread manufacturers provide guidance as to the weight that the thread will support.

Heavy stone beads need to be balanced with heavy duty findings and a stringing material that is designed to take the weight of the beads.

Make your beads appear to float by using transparent or very fine stringing materials.

Face shape

It's not just the shape of beads that is important when designing jewellery, you also need to consider the different face shapes and hairstyles of the potential wearers. Here are some tips that will help you to choose the right jewellery for each different shape of face: You don't have to completely stick to the shape and size tips as some people can carry off any type of jewellery. Feel free to experiment if it feels right.

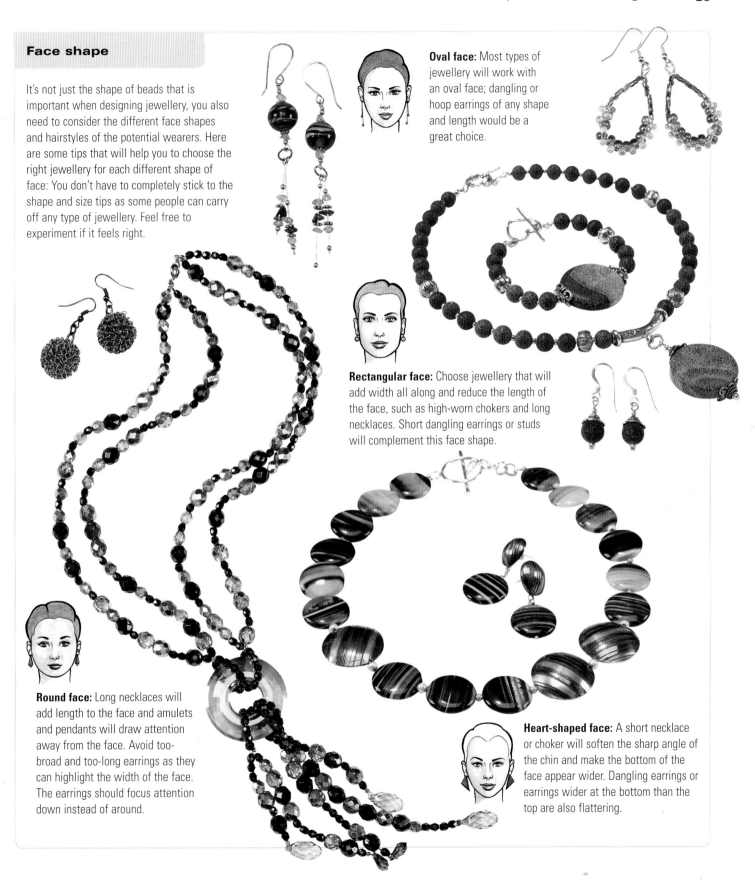

Oval face: Most types of jewellery will work with an oval face; dangling or hoop earrings of any shape and length would be a great choice.

Rectangular face: Choose jewellery that will add width all along and reduce the length of the face, such as high-worn chokers and long necklaces. Short dangling earrings or studs will complement this face shape.

Round face: Long necklaces will add length to the face and amulets and pendants will draw attention away from the face. Avoid too-broad and too-long earrings as they can highlight the width of the face. The earrings should focus attention down instead of around.

Heart-shaped face: A short necklace or choker will soften the sharp angle of the chin and make the bottom of the face appear wider. Dangling earrings or earrings wider at the bottom than the top are also flattering.

Texture and finishes

Beads come in a variety of textures and finishes. They can be smooth or rough, glossy or matt, dyed or natural, and many more variations. You can add texture to your jewellery by mixing different finishes of beads together. For example, try smooth with rough, or mixing other materials with beads, such as wire and leather. Whatever the combination, you will end up with unique-looking jewellery. Adding texture to your design can change the whole look of your project.

Bead finishes

The surface finish of a bead will greatly influence its colour and therefore its effect in a design. Matt beads absorb light, while shiny beads reflect light and sparkle. Mixing finishes in one piece is a great way to add texture and variation to a design.

1 Transparent finish: These beads transmit light, and you can see through them clearly. This means that their colours tend not to be intense unless they are placed against a background.

2 Translucent finish: These beads also transmit light; you can see through them a little but not clearly. They have a more muted appearance than transparent beads.

3 Opal finish: These beads transmit some light, but have a very milky finish. They tend to have a subtle and muted appearance.

4 Opaque finish: These beads don't transmit light; you cannot see through them. They are bold in colour and design and would leap out if part of a design.

All the available textures and finishes are combined into this necklace, and the design works as a whole.

TIP: DESIGN

As beaders and jewellery makers we're often drawn to shiny things, but beware of using too much shine in your pieces. When the eye sees something shiny, it can be overwhelming; the eye immediately searches for something matt. If you don't include anything matt, people's eyes may get restless and they will not see the true beauty of your work.

5 Satin finish: These beads are silky to the touch and very tactile. They are versatile and blend well with both matt and gloss beads. Don't let them come into contact with perfume or alcohol.

6 Metallic finish: These beads are shiny, with a galvanized (coated) finish, which may wear off over time. Metallic finishes add a sense of luxury and glitz to a design.

7 Matt finish: These beads are non-gloss or frosted and will tend to recede into the background rather than jump out.

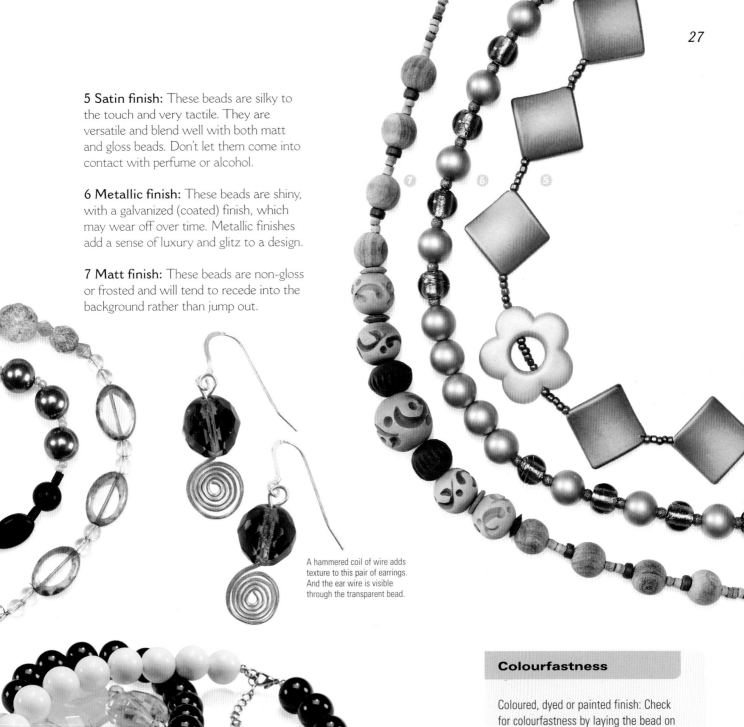

A hammered coil of wire adds texture to this pair of earrings. And the ear wire is visible through the transparent bead.

This black and white necklace combines gloss, opaque, transparent and opal beads to dramatic effect.

Colourfastness

Coloured, dyed or painted finish: Check for colourfastness by laying the bead on a white dampened cloth or absorbent cotton. Make sure that dyed beads don't stain your clothes and that they are not going to be worn close to areas where lotion, hairspray, perfume or perspiration may be present.

Designing with wire and beads

Wire brings an exciting dimension to bead jewellery design. Wire is a highly versatile material being attractive, practical, readily available, and easy to work with. There are many types of wire suitable for bead jewellery, including colourful craft wires and wires formed from precious metals. The look and feel of a jewellery design can be altered completely by using a different colour or thickness of wire.

Create eye-catching jewellery with even the plainest of beads by adding decorative wire elements. Simple wire scroll components transform these plain beads into stylish earrings.

When stringing beads, loop the wire around the bead and back through to create a decorative looped effect.

Wire findings

Wire is great for making your own findings and this is ideal if you are looking for something a little different or you want to create your own custom fittings. Many different types of findings can be made with wire including headpins, earrings, rings and bails. Create designs that make a feature of your findings, for instance a wire clasp that becomes a stunning focal point for your jewellery piece or decorative chains that add an ornate flourish to your designs. Select wire that complements or contrasts with the other materials in your designs.

Wire for decorative bead stringing

Make wire a feature of your designs by stringing the wire so that some of it is left exposed. Consider alternative ways of using wire as a stringing material, perhaps by running the wire through the bead twice and exploring creative ways of displaying the exposed wire. This is a great way to add interest to plain beads. Use coloured wire to bring a playful look to your designs or traditional silver or gold for a more classic feel.

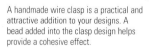

A handmade wire clasp is a practical and attractive addition to your designs. A bead added into the clasp design helps provide a cohesive effect.

Use coloured wires of varying thickness to create a wide variety of spacer beads. With so many different colours of wire available you can create decorative elements to complement your colour scheme.

TIP: WIRE

Coloured craft wire is typically coated copper wire. This coating can wear away against the rough edges of beads. This will expose the copper, which may tarnish.

Which type of wire?

When you incorporate wire into your jewellery designs there are some important things to consider:

Cost: The metal that the wire is made from will help to determine the cost. Precious metal wire is more costly than copper or craft wire. Consider precious metal plated or filled wire as a cost-effective alternative.

Diameter: Make sure that the wire is the right diameter for your beads. If you are using wire as a stringing material, this means it should be thick enough to hold its shape but not so thick that it won't thread through the beads.

Quality: If possible try to match the quality of the beads with the quality of the wire. Use silver or gold-fill wire with high-quality beads.

Decorative wire elements

Add decorative elements to your jewellery designs using wire. Interesting spacers made from coils of wire or decorative bails that are a stunning feature in their own right can be formed from wire using just basic wire working techniques. One of the benefits of designing jewellery that uses wire elements is that you can create completely custom components that will really make your designs stand out. Use coloured craft wire to make decorative elements that harmonize with your bead choice.

TIP: WIRE

Wires are often sold in different states of hardness. Soft wire is often best for projects that require a lot of twisting and manipulation.

Wire wrapping

Use simple wire wrapping techniques to add texture and dimension to your beads. Wrapping a bead with wire is a great way to make a feature bead and focal point for a jewellery design. The intricate look of a wire-wrapped bead is enhanced when using silver wire that is oxidized to darken parts of the wire surface.

Wire is difficult and sometimes impossible to reuse. Practice with low cost craft wires if you are new to working with wire. This is a good way to try new ideas without the risk of wasting expensive materials.

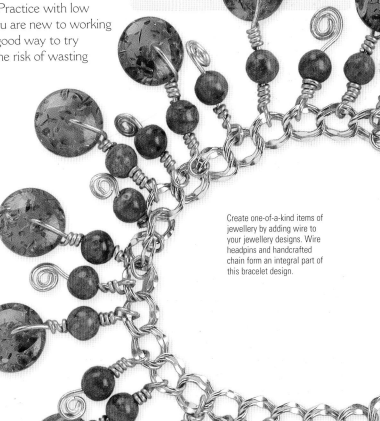

Create one-of-a-kind items of jewellery by adding wire to your jewellery designs. Wire headpins and handcrafted chain form an integral part of this bracelet design.

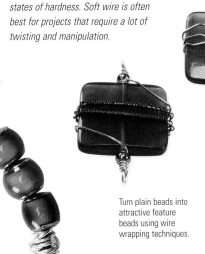

Turn plain beads into attractive feature beads using wire wrapping techniques.

Accents, features, patterns and repeats

Use design techniques such as accents, patterns and repeats to make your jewellery designs really pop. A few well-placed accents or a simple repeat pattern can make your jewellery really stand out.

Accents and features

Use accents and features as highlights in your jewellery, to draw the eye to specific aspects, or to break up large expanses of a similar colour or pattern. To make your accents eye-catching, ensure that they really stand out from the rest of the piece by choosing different sizes, contrasting colours, alternative textures or introducing something completely different such as a striking feature bead, charm or decorative clasp. Use your stringing material to add interest to your jewellery. Tie knots in ribbons or cord to create an interesting alternative to spacer beads.

Use feature beads to transform an otherwise plain piece of jewellery. A feature bead can be used in a variety of ways. Hang the bead pendant-like from a beaded necklace or choose a feature bead that you can thread into your design. One of the benefits of introducing feature beads to your work is that you can include beads, such as designer lampwork beads or hand crafted metal clay beads, that may be cost prohibitive to use in bulk.

Feature beads – like this centre-front pendant – break up the pattern and add a focal point to a design.

A feature bead that mimics the shape and size of the rest of the beads creates a point of interest without detracting from the design. The silver cylinder spacers echo the brushed silver of the feature bead.

Larger accent beads are used to add interest to this necklace without overpowering the smaller seed beads.

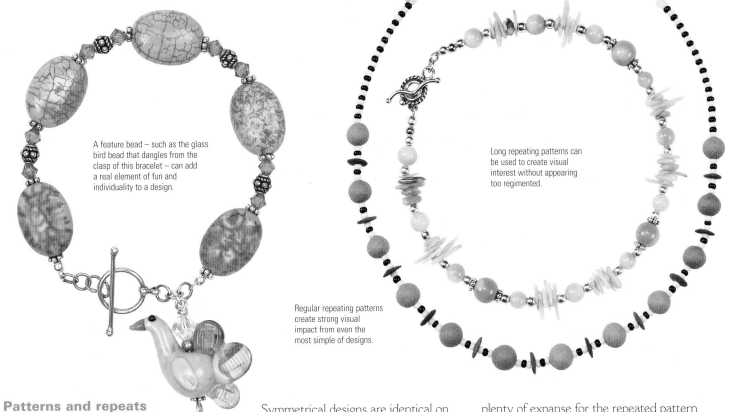

A feature bead – such as the glass bird bead that dangles from the clasp of this bracelet – can add a real element of fun and individuality to a design.

Regular repeating patterns create strong visual impact from even the most simple of designs.

Long repeating patterns can be used to create visual interest without appearing too regimented.

Patterns and repeats

Combine colours and shapes of beads together to create a pattern in your design. Patterns give you a wealth of creative opportunities and allow you to stamp your identity on your work. The same beads can be used to create symmetrical, asymmetrical, formal, semiformal or random designs simply by varying the order that you string the beads and the combinations used.

Symmetrical designs are identical on both sides, so that one is a mirror image of the other. An asymmetrical design is different on each side. This can be a striking design technique, however it can be difficult to get right. The balance of the piece may be altered by the fact that the design is not the same on both sides.

Formal patterns are created by repeating the stringing order of beads. This works best on larger pieces as this allows plenty of expanse for the repeated pattern to be displayed.

When you are designing the pattern to incorporate into your jewellery you will need to consider the size and shape of the finished piece as well as that of the individual beads. A beading board is the perfect tool for experimentation, allowing you to create different patterns and combinations quickly and easily.

Being random

Producing successful random patterns is surprisingly difficult. Get it wrong and the end result looks like a mismatch of beads. Get it right, however, and you will create a stunning and eclectic piece of jewellery. A little planning will go a long way towards ensuring great looking random results:

- Ensure that the beads are united in some way. Pick beads that are the same colour, a similar shade or share the same design style. This will pull the piece together even though the pattern is random.
- Divide your beads into equal parts and string one part at a time. This will ensure that the beads are equally distributed even though the stringing is random.
- Consider the finished effect. Very small beads strung randomly, for instance, will blend when viewed from a distance to create a new colour.

Random designs, mixing pattern, texture and colour, give jewellery a playful look.

Design styles

The earliest forms of jewellery were made from bones, shells and seeds. Special pieces, often with particular significance, were worn on various parts of the body such as the head/hair, neck, arms/hands, body and legs/feet. Nowadays, jewellery has become more of a style statement and can complement your outfits or bring out your personality. It can be made from a huge range of materials with unique designs. Non-jewellery items, such as charms and bookmarks, are also created using similar techniques.

BANGLES

Bangles are bracelets formed by a single ring with no opening. They may be made from hard material such as wood, wire, plastic or metal.

Jewellery for arms and hands

Because of their simple form and short length in comparison to necklaces, bracelets are very appealing projects to the beginner designer. They offer the opportunity to try out techniques, patterns and colour combinations in a quick-to-make format before you move on to a larger necklace project.

Rings offer slightly more of a challenge because they must fit exactly to the finger. Ring shanks can be bought and embellished or made from wire or beads as a part of whole design. Adjustable ring shanks are available to buy.

MEMORY WIRE BRACELET

For a memory wire bracelet, beads are threaded onto strong wire that doesn't lose its shape. It's easy to wear, a clasp is not needed and it's a suitable project for an unknown wearer as this style will fit anyone.

RINGS AND TOE RINGS

Beaded rings are fashionable additions to your jewellery collection. They can be made by using wire wrapping techniques or by using prefabricated sieve findings. Toe rings work well with open shoes. They are usually made from metal and can be decorated with stones, beads, crystals or carved designs. They come in different measurements to fit your feet. When designing a toe ring, one of your main considerations should be comfort. The wearer might be on their feet all day and so a toe ring should not chafe and should not be too thick or chunky.

ELASTIC BRACELET

Threading beads onto elastic is the easiest way to make a bracelet, tied with a secure knot. It is comfortable to wear and remove as it's stretchy and can fit any size of wrist. A clasp is not needed, so this is particularly suitable for children's and men's beaded bracelets.

SINGLE- AND MULTISTRAND BRACELETS

Beads threaded onto single- or multi-strand beading wire, closed with a clasp. You need to know the size of the wearer's wrist.

Earrings

Earrings are decorative jewellery for the earlobes. They can be quick-to-make and can accommodate many design options, in terms of both embellishment and findings and fittings. They come in two basic types: pierced and clip-on, and within those types the available styles are studs, drops, dangling, hoops and chandeliers.

DANGLING EARRINGS

Dangling earrings that hang down from the earlobes in different lengths may be quite short or long enough to touch your shoulders. Any type of earring hooks and any kind of material can be used, such as chain, glass, crystal, acrylic or wood.

DROPS

Drop earrings usually have one larger gemstone or bead, a geometric shape or charms hanging from the earring base and facing forwards. They are usually attached to an ear wire rather than a stud.

STUDS

Stud earrings have a 'post', which is a straight piece of wire with a stopper on one end and secured with an ear nut on the other end. Embellishments can be small and static, or chains and other moving items can be attached.

CLIP-ON/SCREW-IN POST

The screw-in post is a clasp mechanism that allows you to adjust the fit of an earring by rotating the earring's backing. Other clip-on earrings may have a spring attachment with a hinged back, so they can be simply snapped onto the earlobe. Magnetic clip-on earrings are also available.

HOOPS

Hoop earrings are circular or oval, and are usually made from fine wire. They come in many sizes, from tiny to shoulder-length. They may be plain (gold or silver) or threaded with beads, charms and other materials. They also may be open and secured with an ear nut or enclosed.

CHANDELIERS

Chandeliers have multilevelled or layered branches that hang down from the main earring base. They often have movement when they dangle.

Collar (30–33cm [12–13in]): Worn tight and high up on the neck, like a dog collar. Usually multistrand, not recommended for people who are not comfortable wearing tight items around their neck.

Choker (35–40cm [14–16in]): Fits very tightly around neck, lower down, just above the collarbone. Usually single-strand, suitable for formal and informal occasions.

Princess (43–48cm [17–19in]): The most popular length of necklace sits high on the chest, and is great with pendants.

Matinee (50–63cm [20–25in]): Worn down to the breastbone; suitable for casual or business wear.

Opera (66–91cm [26–36in]): Elegant and sophisticated, but draws attention down to the chest.

Rope (over 114cm [over 45in]): Draws attention to torso as it's quite long, but it can be shortened by double-or multi-stranding or by being knotted in front.

Lariat (over 114cm [over 45in]): Lariats are unattached at one end and so are worn knotted at the front. They can be knotted just once or multiple times and using different knots for different decorative effects.

Standard necklace lengths

The names of the standard necklace lengths come from a long tradition going back many years. Their names reflect the occasions on which it was once thought appropriate to wear them. Today, they are a useful guide to the bead jewellery designer when planning a piece, or when designing for a specific person.

DROP-CRYSTAL LARIAT
Lariats are unique among necklaces because they are not joined with a clasp. This multistrand lariat takes advantage of this feature by incorporating AB-coated drop crystals into the design on the knotted ends of the necklace.

Non-jewellery beaded and wired objects

Beading and wire techniques can be used to create non-jewellery items such as charms, tassel clips, decorated fabrics, wineglass charms, bookmarks, wire-beaded decorations and many more.

ANKLETS

Anklets are pieces of jewellery worn on the ankle. Anklets can be made from different materials such as beads, wood, leather, fabric, metal wire or chains. Anklets are usually larger than bracelets and would probably be too large to wear on the wrist; however some bracelets, as long as they're not too bulky, can easily be worn on the ankle. Slender necklaces could also be worn on the ankle if they wrapped around more than once.

WINEGLASS CHARMS

Wineglass charms are small beaded wire rings attached to the stem of a wine or champagne glass. They are not just designed to complement your glass at a dinner table or party, but also identify which glass belongs to you. Small earring hooks with loops can be used for making glass charms. This is a good way of using up leftover beads and pieces of wire.

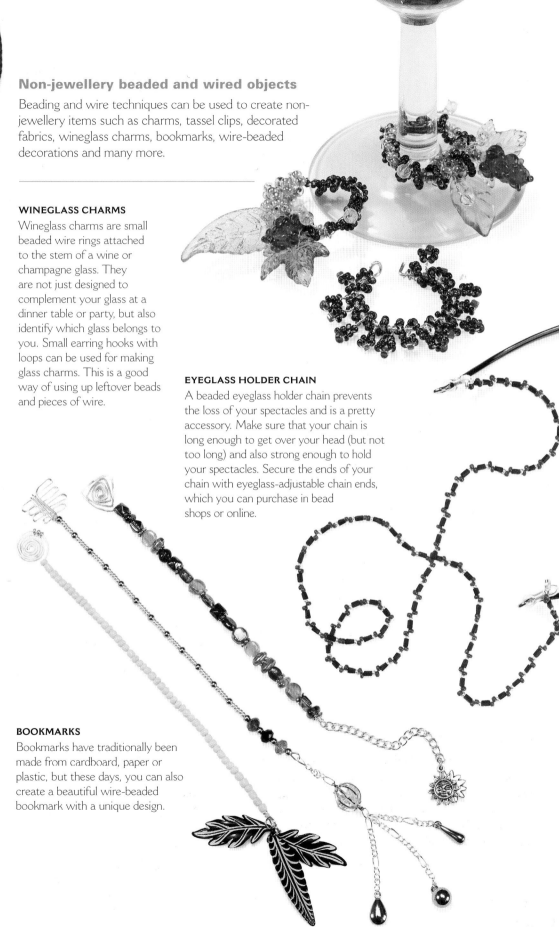

EYEGLASS HOLDER CHAIN

A beaded eyeglass holder chain prevents the loss of your spectacles and is a pretty accessory. Make sure that your chain is long enough to get over your head (but not too long) and also strong enough to hold your spectacles. Secure the ends of your chain with eyeglass-adjustable chain ends, which you can purchase in bead shops or online.

BROOCHES

Brooches are pieces of jewellery with a long tradition and are also known as decorative pins. These days you don't have to wear them in a traditional way on the collar of your jacket, but you can wear them as an extravagant accessory elsewhere, for example on the waistline, as a purse ornament, on your hat or belt, and anywhere else you can think of.

BOOKMARKS

Bookmarks have traditionally been made from cardboard, paper or plastic, but these days, you can also create a beautiful wire-beaded bookmark with a unique design.

Simply beads

Beads are decorative objects pierced and ready for threading, stitching or wiring. They can be made out of any material, natural or manmade, and are available in a huge variety of colours, shapes, textures and price ranges. Choosing the right beads for your design can be a confusing process. Over the course of this chapter the individual types of beads are presented and discussed in detail – organized into types according to the material they are made from – providing all you need to know to help you choose the right beads for your projects.

Buying beads

Be prepared to be overwhelmed, especially if you are visiting a bead shop for the first time. If you are going to purchase particular beads or findings, make a list before you visit the shop. Otherwise you risk getting so excited about all those beautiful beads around you that you forget to buy what you went there for in the first place.

It is good to have a design in mind so you don't get too carried away when buying beads. Building a design simply around finding beads you like can be fun, but it can also turn out to be expensive! Try to be disciplined.

TIP: BUYING BEADS
Don't reuse the thread from strung beads as it is usually cheap and for display purposes only.

Nylon beading thread

Buyers' notes
Walking into a bead shop is like walking into an Aladdin's cave or sweet shop – you feel slightly confused because you want to buy everything all at the same time. If you are shopping for particular beads or findings, make a list before you visit the shop to make sure that you get the beads that you need. It is good to have a design in mind so that you don't get too carried away when buying beads.

Don't be afraid to ask
Don't be afraid to ask for help from the staff working at the shop. They will be happy to help you and they are always very knowledgeable about their stock and beading techniques.

Buying beads online
Buying beads online is quick and easy and you can do it from the comfort of your own home. The main drawbacks are that you can't check the bead sizes carefully (see size charts on pages 137–138) and that you risk ending up with poor-quality beads. Buying beads online obviously takes away your ability to handle the beads, but if the bead description is good and the picture is clear, then you shouldn't have any problems.

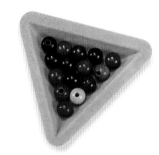

BASKETS, TRAYS AND PENS
Try to walk around the entire shop before you start shopping – that way you can get an overview of the stock. You will find little baskets or trays with plastic bags and pens lying around. These are there for you to put your beads in before you get to the till. The pens are for you to write down the prices of individual loose beads – for example, if you are buying five beads and they cost 50 pence each, then you can keep track of the total cost on the plastic bag.

TIP: BUYING BEADS
Before you remove your beads from the packaging to shop, remember to make a note of the shop contact details in case you would like to purchase the same beads again in the future.

Seed beads in set quantities, and displayed in packets.   Larger beads displayed in wooden trays.

Semiprecious stones and feature beads are often supplied on strings.

FINDING THE RIGHT BEADS

The beads are usually laid out by type and colour; going by the colour is probably the easiest way. Loose beads will be displayed in open trays with the prices stated on each compartment. Seed beads and fine-cut crystal beads can be found in plastic tubes/boxes or plastic bags and will be sold by weight. Semiprecious stones, pearls, ceramic beads and some glass beads and crystals can usually be found in strands hanging on the walls.

Bead fairs

If there is not a bead shop near to you, then the best way to find suppliers is to visit a bead fair. This way you can meet many suppliers and you can see in person the type and quality of the beads that they sell. You can also compare prices between suppliers in one go.

Seeing so many suppliers in one place can be overwhelming, so it is best to first walk through the whole bead fair, then sit down for a cup of tea or coffee to mull things over. Then go back and purchase your beads. Make a list of what kinds of beads and findings you need for your project before you visit the bead fair or shop. You'll always buy more than you've anticipated, but with a shopping list you won't forget to buy the important items that you really came for. Always make sure that you take some cash with you as some of the suppliers will not take credit cards.

The majority of suppliers have their own online shops, so if you would like to use them again in the future, just take their business cards home with you.

Many bead fairs will also feature free demonstrations or workshops and many suppliers will have very good bead deals for fair customers. You can find out about bead fairs by searching on Google, in beading magazines, in bead shops or on your current suppliers' websites.

Storage

Once you have purchased your beads you need to find a solution to store them. Beads can be divided into types or into colours, whichever you prefer. Here are some of the many examples of bead-storage solutions you might come across:

Will you be beading in one room or at a bead group or class? Will you be storing small seed beads or large gemstones, big reels of wire and tools or small reels of thread and packs of needles? How about decanting your beads? Or finding them a home in a see-through case, to avoid opening the lids or reading the labels? Pick and choose from these storage options to suit your beads.

HOMEMADE
You may find that you don't need to purchase storage at all. Camera film containers, glass and plastic bottles, flip-top sweet packets and food storage containers can work just as well as dedicated bead containers.

STORING BEADS

1. Storage jars – several see-through jars that fit together by screwing onto each other; the final jar in the set is secured with a lid. They come in different sizes.

2. Storage trays – come in different sizes and colours but the majority of them are clear with individual compartments and a lid. Some have secure-fastening or individual locking compartments.

3. Hinged boxes – clear boxes with a top lid, suitable for small and delicate beads.

4. Clear plastic tubes – these come with a lid and hanging loop. They come in different sizes, and are suitable for small or delicate beads.

5. Stackable storage ring – usually eight individual compartments in a ring, with snapping lids. A storage ring can act as a mini-organizer.

6. Empty coffee jars – an inexpensive way to shop large numbers of beads.

HOW TO ORGANIZE YOUR BEADS

When planning your storage, you'll need to bear in mind how you want to organize and separate your beads. Do you want to organize them by size? Shape? Colour? Material? These decisions will affect the storage you choose.

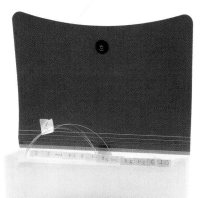

STORAGE CASES

These usually come with removable trays with individual compartments, carry handles and secure fastenings. Storage cases are suitable for travelling and taking your project work securely with you.

TOOL STORAGE

Keeping your tools safely stored where they won't get damaged (or damage anything else) is important. A paintbrush holder, available from art suppliers, is a handy solution for holding pliers, wire cutters and scissors.

WIRE

An expanding file is perfect for holding all your pieces of wire. Separate them by size and type.

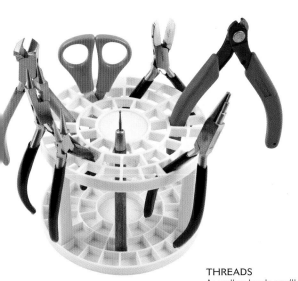

THREADS

As well as beads, you'll need to work out a solution to store all of those extras such as threads. You could keep a range of bobbins on a large stitch holder, usually used in knitting, so they're always handy.

Wooden beads

Wooden beads are the oldest and most natural types of beads, used throughout history around the world. Because of their simplicity, wooden beads are – incorrectly – taken for granted.

Wooden beads are part of the 'natural' bead family, which includes bamboo, coconut, seeds, nuts, shell, horn, bone, stones, pearls and semiprecious beads. These are the obvious choices for combination with wooden beads – but all kinds of beads will work well with wood because they come in an infinite range of colours and shapes. Wooden beads can be found in any bead shop and, as they are cheap, they are a great bead to use when you first get started.

ACCENT BEADS

• *You can create a simple pattern by using two different coloured beads and repeating them all the way around a design.*

• *If you want to be more adventurous, you could repeat the colours – but mix up the sizes and shapes – starting with the smaller beads and progressing to the larger beads in the centre. Using sizes in this order ensures an even balance.*

• *Accent beads can draw out a pattern. In the bracelets shown above, smaller accent beads help to draw out the larger beads.*

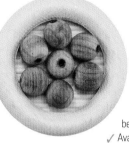

Natural beads (unvarnished)

✓ The most basic wooden bead can be the most attractive.

✓ Available in a range of different shapes and sizes.

✓ Easily decorated with paint or varnishes.

✗ May chip, stain or change shape because they are not varnished.

✗ Sharp material like chain or heavy wire can damage the shape of the bead.

◎ Ribbon, leather, elastic and soft cord.

Matt painted beads (unvarnished)

✓ Matt colours are soft with a satin finish.

✓ Can be used on their own or to help unite strong, shiny beads.

✗ May leave stains on your clothes or body – depending on paint quality. Test them for colourfastness with a damp cloth first to be safe.

◎ Leather, cords, ribbons, elastic, memory wire and beading wire.

REPEAT ONE COLOUR

• *If you want to use lots of different coloured beads together, it is best to separate each bead with a single colour of bead. In this example a small turquoise bead has been used between each larger bead. This helps prevent the colours from clashing and helps you use lots of different colours in the same design. This approach helps you break the colour wheel rules!*

Glazed painted beads (varnished)

✓ Different shapes and sizes – the most used wooden bead.

✓ Long lasting as they are protected by paint and glaze.

✗ Need to use bead caps when stringing with a chain as the chain edges can damage them.

◎ Leather, chain, cords, ribbons, elastic, memory wire and beading wire.

Multicoloured and hand-painted

✓ Bright colours and bold patterns – great for children's jewellery.

✗ Need to keep in mind safety considerations with children's jewellery.

◎ Elastic, soft cords, ribbons, leather and memory wire.

MIXING COLOUR AND SHAPE

• *Mixing colours can be fun and eye-catching, but to ensure they work well together you should pick colours that do not clash and sit naturally together (see Colour essentials, page 10).*

Bead facts

Top properties
° Wooden beads are generally inexpensive, light and versatile.
° They are easy to mix with other types of beads and can also be used as spacer beads.
° Popular with children and suitable for male jewellery.
° Usually they have large holes, so they are easy to use with different types of threading materials including leather, ribbon, cords and elastic.

Finishes
° Natural, matt, glazed, smooth, carved, coloured, hand-painted, dyed or covered with other materials such as cord or fabric.

Materials
° Hardwood (broadleaf trees) such as birch, maple, walnut and fruit trees.
° Softwood (evergreen) trees such as pine and fir.
° Also olive, palm trees and many more.

Colours
° Natural, light, dark, metallic and both subdued and the brightest colours.
° Wooden beads come in a range of solid colours and patterned finishes.
° Commonly seen with the bright colours of African tribal jewellery.

Shapes
° Often round in shape, other common styles include oval, flat, cylinder, disk, rice, square, barrels, tubes, cubes, dice, ring, heart, geometric shapes and carved figurative shapes and objects.

Care
° Wood is a natural and hard wearing product, but sometimes wooden beads chip or lose colour, although this may add to their charm.
° Varnish can make them last longer.
° They can be cleaned with non-chemical soap or tea tree oil if necessary.

Metallic finish
✓ Metallic beads can enhance and visually lift a design.
✓ Can be used to replace heavier metal beads.
✓ Suitable for making even the most glamorous evening jewellery.
✗ Any scratches will be easily noticed.
◉ Leather, cords, elastic, ribbons, memory wire and beading wire.

Carved
✓ Different colours, shapes and sizes.
✓ Come in a variety of unusual shapes, but the most common ones are hearts, animals, letters and symbols.
✓ Can be used to make unique designs.
✗ You need to know your recipient. What do they like, and when will they wear it?
◉ Leather, cords, elastic, ribbons, memory wire and beading wire.

SCALE, PROPORTION AND WEIGHT
● Geometric shaped beads look very heavy, but generally they are very light to wear, made out of light wood.
● Larger pieces of jewellery are generally better suited to people with an outgoing personality, as they are big and bold.
● Chunky, colourful geometric beads look good with summer outfits.

Hand-painted
✓ They make surprising and stunning jewellery.
✓ Usually come in large sizes but they are really lightweight to wear.
✗ Make sure that you don't use too many different patterns in one go as it can make a design look messy.
◉ Leather, cords, elastic, ribbons, memory wire and beading wire.

Geometric shapes
✓ Large-size geometric shaped beads make beautiful chunky bracelets.
✓ They are unusual and light to wear.
✗ Some people will find the largest sizes uncomfortable.
◉ Leather, cords, elastic, ribbons, memory wire and beading wire.

DEFINE THE LOOK (BELOW)
● This Africa-influenced necklace has a clearly defined style with brightly coloured red beads, cream highlights and black knotted cords.
● This asymmetric mix of patterned beads breaks the rules (see Glass beads, page 44). Rules are meant to be broken as they say! However, although you are mixing different beads together, you should still try and use materials and colours that do not clash and that will not break the style (such as a pastel-coloured bead or large blown-glass bead with this necklace). For example, try to mix just natural beads together in your piece.

Glass beads

Glass beads are probably the most well-known types of beads, and they are available in many different colours, shapes and sizes. They may be made by machine or by hand. Unlike machine-made beads, handmade beads are unique (no two are alike) and therefore more expensive.

One of the popular old techniques of hand-making glass beads is lampworking. In this process, beads are formed by melting coloured glass rods over an open flame (torch), wrapped around a thin metal mandrel. The bead is then cooled down slowly in the kiln or in a fibre blanket. It is important to cool glass beads down slowly, as uneven fast cooling can make them crack or break. A good-quality glass bead shouldn't break or crack easily if dropped.

PRESSED GLASS BEADS

- *Using pressed glass beads in one colour but in different shapes can make a stunning piece of jewellery.*
- *The necklace could be fully beaded or partially beaded – where beading wire is visible as a part of the design.*

Handmade lampwork glass beads

✓ A range of individually crafted beads with many colours, shapes, finishes and textures.
✓ Some larger beads can be used as a focal point.
✗ They need a lot of skill to make and it's difficult to manufacture them.
✗ They may crack or break easily if uneven fast cooling is applied during the making process.
✗ As they are unique, they are more expensive than most other beads.
◉ Ribbon, leather, chain, cord and different thicknesses of beading wire.

Venetian (Murano) glass beads

✓ These high-quality beads made in Venice are fashionable and widely recognized.
✓ They come in many unusual colour combinations and finishes, usually influenced by a Venetian artist; therefore a vintage style can be achieved when designing.
✓ Beads can act as a focal point on fabricated threading material.
✓ Murano beads with a sterling silver core are called Pandora-type beads (Pandora beads originated from Denmark).
✗ Not cheap, as lots of craftsmanship involved.
◉ Silver chain and fabrics such as ribbon or silk cord.

HAND-PAINTED GLASS BEADS

- *Multicoloured glass beads are united by a hand-painted design and linked together with a silver chain to form a funky bracelet. The chain could be replaced with a knotted ribbon between the beads.*

FIRE-POLISHED BEADS

- *A sparkle of fire-polished beads gives your jewellery extra texture and individuality.*
- *These beads can stand out on their own or be accompanied by other beads and findings.*

Hand-painted glass beads

✓ Hand-painted beads come in endless variations and create a beautiful effect.
✓ They make fashionable and elegant jewellery.
✓ A single bead can be used as a very interesting focal point.
✗ Over time, some of the bead's decoration may begin to rub off.
◉ Medium or heavy beading wire, coloured choker, chain or cord.

Dichroic and fused glass beads

✓ Dichroic glass beads have a metallic sheen and show two or more colours depending on the angle from which they are viewed.
✓ Fused glass beads are made by placing glass pieces together and fusing them into one smooth piece by heating them in the kiln. Very unusual beads and pendants can be made using this technique.
✓ Both dichroic and fused beads are full of light and change colour when the glass moves – suitable for making special-occasion jewellery.
✗ Some pendants can be quite heavy.
◉ Medium or heavy beading wire, chain, silk or cord.

Bead facts

Top properties
○ Many types of glass beads are available on the market in different price ranges, from cheap to very expensive.
○ They are easy to mix with other types of beads and different stringing materials.
○ Glass beads are suitable for making everyday jewellery or for special occasions.
○ They are long lasting.

Finishes
○ Transparent, translucent, frosted, opal, opaque, matt, glossy, metallic and hand-painted.

Materials
○ Recycled glass.
○ Coloured glass rods.
○ High-quality glass and minerals (minerals enhance colour).

Colours
○ A huge range of colours – light or dark, clear, white or black, gold and silver and many more.
○ Artistic spectrum of colours on handmade beads.

Shapes
○ Common shapes are round and oval but others are available: cube, barrel, disk, bicone, drop, nugget, heart, chip, doughnut, rectangle (regular and irregular), rondelle, triangle and tube.

Care
○ Over time glass beads can become cloudy and dusty. To bring back their shine, place an old towel at the bottom of the sink (to avoid scratching your beads) and soak the beads in mild soapy water for a few minutes. Dry the beads thoroughly using a soft towel.

Millefiori glass beads
✓ Millefiori beads are made up of sliced cane (a bit like a stick of rock) with many different patterns, designs and multiple colours (millefiori translates as 'thousand flowers').
✓ Millefiori beads are very affordable and come in many different shapes and sizes.
✓ A colourful range of jewellery can be made from millefiori beads, such as pendants, rings and earrings.
✗ Due to the nature of handmade beads, the sizes and colours of the beads may vary.
◉ Heavy beading wire for large beads, fine cord or elastic for lighter beads.

Czech faceted and fire-polished glass beads
✓ The faceted effect is achieved by chipping glass around the edges to transmit light in many directions; the most popular faceted beads are Czech fire-polished glass beads.
✓ Fire-polished beads are affordable and add sophistication to a design because of their high reflection.
✓ Beads come in various shapes, sizes and types of coatings and can be complemented with semiprecious stones, silver and other glass beads.
✓ Long-lasting beads – the colour won't fade or chip off.
✗ Beads may get a little dusty or cloudy and need to be cleaned often with a damp cloth.
◉ Light, medium or heavy beading wire; cords, ribbons, chain and elastic.

AFRICAN GLASS BEADS
○ Analogous yellow and green colours (see Colour schemes, page 11) blend to give this necklace a warm feel.
○ To keep the natural and warm look of these Ghanaian beads, thread them onto a cotton cord or other natural threading material.
○ This could work as a short or long necklace with the larger bead used to make a central focal point.

SILVER FOIL TWISTED GLASS PENDANT
○ The green silver foil twisted glass pendant is made with a combination of transparent glass and silver foil, shaped into a drop with a twisted end.
○ A simple but elegant design can be achieved by placing a pendant on a coloured wire choker, cord or leather thong.

Pressed glass beads
✓ Pressed glass beads are made by using one of the oldest techniques, pouring hot glass into moulds to form the beads into regular shapes and sizes.
✓ Pressed glass beads can be transparent or translucent, they also come in many colours.
✓ They are cost-effective and open to many design possibilities.
✗ Cheaper pressed glass beads can have uneven holes, so try to get hold of good-quality ones such as Czech pressed glass beads.
◉ Light, medium and heavy beading wire; chain, ribbon and cord.

African glass beads
✓ African glass beads are made from melted coloured recycled glass (ground down to powder form) and fused again into solid glass. They come in various shapes and are decorated with distinctive coloured patterns.
✓ Contrasting colours of beads sometimes represent symbolic or community values; designing with these beads can be a slightly different challenge.
✗ Recycled glass beads may be passed off as genuine African trade beads – obviously there is a big difference in price and authenticity!
◉ Cotton cord, leather, suede.

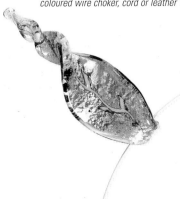

Ceramic and polymer clay beads

Ceramic beads are made from ceramic clay, hand-formed into shape, moulded or carved, and then heated to a high temperature in a kiln before being decorated. Often, ceramic beads change colour after firing. Different finishes may be applied – they may be left unglazed, glazed, crackle-glazed or painted. Porcelain is a particular kind of white clay that comes from China.

Polymer clay is an easy-to-use craft material and is much more versatile than ceramic or porcelain. It is odourless and it doesn't dry out, so you can easily make your own beads and you don't need a kiln for firing polymer clay; you can do it in an ordinary oven. The colour and size of the material will not change during the firing process. You can blend two or more colours together to get a different appearance and the different brands of polymer clay can also be mixed.

MIXED POLYMER CLAY AND CERAMIC BEADS
○ *Many polymer clay beads come in funky designs and therefore they are popular for making children's jewellery.*
○ *Mixing polymer clay and ceramic beads can make for a beautiful project. They can also be mixed with other types of beads.*

KASHMIRI BEADS
○ *Kashmiri beads have an exotic look. They are made from polymer clay and are designed to look like traditional Indian 'Lac' beads, which are made from a natural resin.*
○ *When designing, work out a pattern or just use these beads randomly – they will work well either way.*

Unglazed ceramic beads
✓ They have been fired once (in a technique known as bisque firing) but they still offer a solid, good-value bead.
✓ Unglazed beads can be further glazed or painted.
✓ An excellent basis for all design ideas.
✗ These beads should be handled with care; if too much pressure is applied they may crack.
◎ Heavy or medium string, hemp, cord and leather.

Glazed ceramic beads
✓ Different types of glaze have been applied, such as metallic, crackle, rough finish (aka. raku) or splash dye.
✓ These are smooth and colourful beads or pendants, and come in different shapes and sizes.
✓ Glazed beads can be used in combination with other types of beads.
✗ These beads can be quite heavy.
◎ Hemp, cord and leather.

Hand-painted ceramic beads
✓ Hand-painted ceramic beads and pendants can add eye-catching detail to your jewellery designs.
✓ Beads come in vibrant colours and patterns, and may be easily used as a focal point or mixed with other beads.
✗ Sometimes the size or pattern will vary noticeably – although this could be a good thing, depending upon your design.
◎ Hemp, cord and leather.

POLYMER CLAY TEXTURES
○ *Combining smooth and rough textures in a piece can work very well, as shown by this elastic polymer clay bead bracelet.*

Kashmiri polymer clay beads
✓ A traditonal-style of handmade Indian bead.
✓ Kashmiri beads are made from polymer clay with metal holes and are hand decorated with seed beads, stones, glitter, mirror chips, glass, crystal, fabrics, resin, metal, wire and more.
✓ The individual finish of Kashmiri beads gives a unique look to your project and you will end up with a truly original piece of jewellery.
✗ Some of the heavy bead decorations may wear off, so make sure you get good-quality beads.
◎ Silk, ribbon, chain, cord and leather.

Bead facts

Top properties

∘ Ceramic and polymer clay beads come in vibrant colours, patterns, shapes and sizes and look good as a focal point of the jewellery.
∘ These beads are very affordable and easily available.
∘ Many different stringing materials can be used for ceramic and polymer clay beads.
∘ These beads are easy to mix with other types of beads.
∘ The making process of polymer clay beads is reasonably easy and you can do it yourself at home.
∘ Colourful, funky and arty beads and pendants can be made out of polymer clay.

Finishes

∘ Glazed or unglazed, hand-painted or plain, transparent or translucent, smooth or rough, bright or less bright, solid or delicate, marble or semiprecious stone effect, metallic or carved.

Materials

∘ Ceramic or porcelain.
∘ Odourless polymer clay.

Colors

∘ A rich colour palette, including translucent and metallic.
∘ Marble and abstract effects and patterns can be achieved by mixing colours together.

Shapes

∘ Round and oval, rectangle, triangle, square, tube, barrel, abacus, disk, teardrop, butterfly, other shapes such as animals.

Care

∘ Beads can be wiped with a microfibre cloth to remove dust.
∘ If additional cleaning is needed (to remove dirt) rinse beads in hot water and dry completely with a microfibre cloth.

Moulded glazed ceramic beads

✓ Moulded glazed beads come in different colours, shapes and sizes with the opportunity for unique results.
✓ These beads usually come with a thicker coating, offering more protection or different textures to use in your designs.
✓ Moulded beads can come in basic shapes but also in a range of different forms such as animals, flowers, hearts and other more unusual shapes.
✗ The weight of the beads varies, therefore a strong stringing material is required.
◉ Hemp, cord and leather.

Carved ceramic beads

✓ Hand-carved ceramic beads and pendants come in lots of different textures.
✓ Carved ceramic bead designs are quite often inspired by art and nature and can include designs such as gods and goddesses, Celtic art, small creatures, leaves, flowers, animals or human figures.
✓ Single pendants hanging on a simple cord wire can look stunning.
✗ Large beads are not suitable for making earrings because of their weight.
◉ Hemp, cord and leather.

MIXED SHAPES, SIZES AND COLOURS
∘ Remember that larger ceramic beads will be heavy, therefore you will have to string them onto strong material – waxed cord in this case.
∘ Combinations of colours should be easy on the eye; the whole piece of jewellery should be visually balanced.

Polymer clay beads

✓ You can make your own polymer clay beads at home. You can buy a premade cane of clay or make your own.
✓ Polymer clay beads are fun to work with and they come in many vibrant colours, shapes, sizes and patterns.
✓ Good-quality polymer clay beads can look just as stylish as other types of beads.
✗ When making beads, follow the instructions carefully to avoid burning them in the oven.
◉ Light and medium beading wire, cord, leather, ribbon, elastic and chain.

Shaped polymer clay beads

✓ Polymer clay can be purchased in many craft shops in a range of different colours and textures.
✓ You can use your creativity to produce unusual beads of many different shapes: flowers, drops, even novelty shapes such as cakes, people and animals.
✓ Funky shaped polymer clay beads are suitable for making simple children's jewellery when threaded onto elastic.
✗ Beads with delicate parts may break if dropped on a hard surface.
◉ Light and medium beading wire, ribbon, elastic, cord and chain.

SINGLE CERAMIC BEAD PENDANT
∘ A large single ceramic bead can be used as a central focal point and main feature.
∘ To enhance this bead/pendant further, use metal beads either side, as shown here.

Semiprecious beads

There are many types of semiprecious beads. For example, pearls and coral are considered semiprecious stones. These 'earthy' gems don't have the shimmer that precious stones (known as gemstones) do, as they have a matt surface, but are still an excellent way of injecting affordable luxury into your designs.

SANDSTONE ON RIBBON
- *The earthy colouring and finish of semiprecious sandstone beads looks lovely threaded onto ribbon and divided with knots.*
- *The smooth texture of the ribbon complements the rough texture of the sandstone beads.*

Semiprecious beads come in all shapes, sizes and colours. Choosing semiprecious stones for your jewellery project can sometimes be difficult, but try to find ones that fit your personality and that you can afford. Semiprecious stones are priced, like precious stones, according to their value. This is judged on criteria, such as the quality of cut, colour, clarity and finish.

Amethyst beads

✓ Amethyst beads come in different sizes, shapes and shades of purple. They look beautiful on their own or may be mixed with other semiprecious stones.

✓ Amethyst chipped-style beads threaded onto elastic can create a simple and beautiful bracelet.

✓ Amethyst beads are affordable and widely available.

✓ Perfect for all design ideas, although silver and black findings or pearls go particularly well with them.

✗ Amethysts can be easily mistaken for fluorite as they look very similar.

◉ Heavy (for larger beads) or medium string, cord, elastic and ribbon.

Malachite beads

✓ Malachite is an opaque stone in many shades of green with irregular black markings and a silky, velvety finish.

✓ Malachite beads have a beautiful marbled effect.

✓ Malachite looks stunning set in silver.

✓ Available in many different shapes and sizes.

✗ Markings (swirls) on handcrafted malachite beads may vary.

◉ Heavy, medium and light beading wire, elastic, cord, leather and chain.

Sandstone beads

✓ Sandstone is a rock formed at the bottom of the ocean and can be found in many colours, but the most common are pink, brown and black.

✓ Various sizes and shapes of sandstone beads are available.

✓ Sandstone beads can be mixed with other beads, but they will work well on their own despite irregular sizes and shapes.

✗ Sandstone is a natural stone but is sometimes mistaken for goldstone; however, goldstone is a manmade semiprecious stone with copper flecks.

◉ Heavy and medium beading wire, elastic, cord, leather and chain.

BIRTHSTONES

Birthstones may be precious stones (such as diamond) or semiprecious stones (such as topaz) associated with a particular month of the year; they also have a symbolic meaning such as love, good luck, fortune and so on. It's believed that you'll get the most benefit from your birthstone by wearing it in your birth month.

Month	Birthstone	Meaning
January	Garnet	Prosperity/health
February	Amethyst	Wisdom/security
March	Aquamarine	Loyalty/happiness
April	Diamond	Clarity/eternal love
May	Emerald	Patience/understanding
June	Pearl/moonstone	Purity/happiness

Month	Birthstone	Meaning
July	Ruby	Love/success
August	Peridot	Fame/protection
September	Sapphire	Truth/commitment
October	Opal	Hope/faith
November	Yellow topaz/citrine	Wisdom/courage
December	Blue topaz/turquoise	True love/success

Bead facts

Top properties

○ Every semiprecious stone has a different metaphysical property and they have many different meanings.

○ Semiprecious beads make unique, attractive and long-lasting jewellery.

○ Easily available within most price ranges.

○ Semiprecious beads are easy to mix and look good set in gold or silver.

○ Different types of threading materials can be used for semiprecious beaded jewellery such as leather, cord, chain, elastic and many more.

○ The stones are cold to the touch when compared to plastic, proving their authenticity.

Finishes

○ Rough, frosted, matt, marble, polished (tumbling is the technique used for smoothing and polishing the stones).

○ Faceting is a skilled stone-cutting technique – usually used for expensive precious stones such as diamonds or more expensive semiprecious stones such as garnet.

Materials

○ Minerals are solid natural formations, such as amethyst.

○ Rocks are combinations of minerals, such as lapis lazuli.

○ Organic materials include amber.

Colours

○ Available in a variety of colours and shades.

○ Semiprecious bead colours are natural or may be altered by dyeing or bleaching.

Shapes

○ Many varieties of shapes, the same as for any other types of beads. However, the small polished drilled chips (leftover pieces) are the cheapest way to work with semiprecious stones.

Care

○ Clean rocks and minerals (such as turquoise and malachite) regularly with a moist cloth, but avoid water or soap (so the stone remains shiny).

○ Organic semiprecious stones (such as amber and coral) – remove dust and oil with a soft cloth.

○ Protect semiprecious stones by storing them in jewellery boxes or in fabric pouches to prevent scratching.

Fluorite beads

✓ This stone is believed to draw off stress and negativity and is also known as the 'genius stone'.

✓ Beads come in different shades of purple, lilac and green.

✓ Both gold and silver findings can be combined with fluorite.

✓ They are easy to mix with other type of beads (especially crystals).

✗ These are often mistaken for amethyst when cut or formed into beads.

◉ Heavy or medium string, cord, elastic, ribbon and chain.

Agate beads

✓ Colourful and clear beads, usually with stunning white markings; black and red agate beads are most common but yellow and green is also available.

✓ You can make stunning and exquisite jewellery with a single agate pendant.

✗ The markings on the beads will vary slightly.

◉ Heavy or medium string, cord, elastic, chain and leather.

Jade beads

✓ Jade beads come in vibrant colours with natural patterning; the colour is affected by elements in the ground. The most common colours are green, shades of red, orange and yellow.

✓ Jade beads can be mixed with other semiprecious beads and finished with gold or silver findings.

✓ The holes on some beads may be drilled with a rough finish; to prevent tearing use strong wire or thread.

✗ Jade is extremely rare and therefore expensive, especially white, violet, and black jade beads.

◉ Heavy or medium string, cord, elastic, chain, leather.

CHAKRA CRYSTALS

Each chakra point has a colour associated with seven energy points running from the head to the base of the spine. Chakra crystals used in jewellery can be used to balance these energy points.

LIME JADE AND LAVA BEADS

○ When designing with large semiprecious beads, keep in mind that they are going to be heavy, and choose strong threading material.

○ If you are going to mix large and heavy semiprecious beads (lime jade) with other semiprecious stones, choose a lighter one such as lava, so you are not adding any more weight to your jewellery.

Black onyx beads

✓ Black onyx can be natural or dyed; it comes in a pure black colour. Onyx stones come in different types and the names of the stones depend on the colour. For example, red onyx is called carnelian.

✓ Black onyx is easy to mix with other semiprecious or precious stones and looks very elegant set in silver or gold. It is very suitable for eveningwear.

✓ Black onyx beads come in different shapes and sizes and are affordable.

✗ The more uniform beads will usually be treated or dyed, so may not look natural.

◎ Heavy, medium and light beading wire; elastic, cord, leather and chain.

Calcite beads

✓ Calcite beads are smooth and elegant and come in several rich colours and shades, such as clear, white, yellow, blue, red, green, brown or a combination of these with striped markings.

✓ Each bead will have individual markings and colouration; together they can make a stunning and unusual piece of jewellery.

✗ Individual colouration and markings may be a problem, depending on your design.

◎ Light and medium beading wire, ribbon, elastic, cord and chain.

MULTISTRAND FRESHWATER PEARLS

• *Threading freshwater pearls onto multiple-strand clear nylon thread will give the optical illusion of pearls floating around your neck; you may not notice the thread at all when looking at the necklace from a distance. This necklace has a romantic and elegant feel.*

Turquoise beads

✓ Turquoise comes in blue, yellow and green shades.

✓ Beads may be plain or have unique brown patterns (matrix) caused by naturally formed veins in the stone.

✓ Turquoise beads are very versatile; larger beads can be used to make pendants.

✓ Turquoise beads are commonly used in silver settings rather than gold, but antique gold will give a slightly vintage look.

✓ They are easy to mix with other semiprecious beads such as amber, pearls and coral.

✗ Markings, sizes and shapes of turquoise beads may vary.

◎ Light and medium beading wire, ribbon, elastic, cord, leather and chain.

Coral beads

✓ Coral comes in different colours (white, pink, orange, red, violet, blue, gold and black) but the most popular is red, or red sponge coral (it has a spongelike appearance).

✓ Coral beads can be cut into different shapes and sizes.

✓ Coral beads are easy to mix with other semiprecious stones and look good set in silver or gold, so they are popular in fashion jewellery.

✗ Dark- and rich-coloured coral is more expensive then the lighter-coloured type.

◎ Medium beading wire, ribbon, elastic, cord, leather and chain.

FLUORITE AND QUARTZ CRYSTAL

• *Using semiprecious drilled and polished chips is the cheapest way to start working with stones.*

• *Mixing drilled chips from different semiprecious stones, as here, can create an interesting piece of jewellery.*

ADDING TEXTURE WITH WIRE AND CHAIN

• *You can create unusual jewellery by wrapping your semiprecious beads with silver wire.*

• *Silver brings out the beauty of the coral shown here.*

• *Silver chain links can add an extra texture to your design.*

Freshwater pearl beads

✓ Freshwater pearls come from freshwater mussels and they belong to the semiprecious bead family. They come in a wide variety of colours – some natural, some dyed.

✓ Pearls come in different sizes and shapes – the most common is a potato shape.

✓ Knots between pearls will keep them from rubbing against each other and will also look good.

✗ Natural-coloured and perfectly shaped pearls are more valuable than altered pearls.

◉ Soft wire, ribbon, elastic, silk thread or nylon.

◉ It is recommended that you re-string your pearls quite often (depending on how frequently you are going to wear them).

Amber beads

✓ Amber is fossilized tree resin in an orange-yellow translucent colour. Most of the highest-quality amber beads come from the Baltic countries.

✓ Amber beads and pendants come in different shapes and sizes and can be highlighted with silver embellishments.

✓ Both chunky and delicate jewellery projects can be made using amber beads.

✓ To reshop shimmer, polish amber beads with soft cloth – use a small drop of olive oil if necessary.

✗ Handcrafted amber beads and pendants are very unique but expensive.

◉ Light and medium beading wire, ribbon, elastic, cord and silver chain.

ROSE QUARTZ

● *Texture is often added by introducing another colour, shape or size of bead – but these beautiful baby-pink rose quartz beads threaded onto elastic add texture just by the way they are put together. No other colour is needed.*

Quartz crystal beads

✓ Quartz crystal beads (also known as rock crystal beads) are beautifully simple beads with lovely clarity.

✓ They are easy to use with any other types of beads.

✓ Quartz crystal can be hand carved into different shapes.

✗ The weight of the beads varies, therefore stronger stringing material will be required for larger beads.

◉ Heavy (for larger beads) or medium string, cord, elastic and chain.

Rose quartz beads

✓ Rose quartz beads come in varying shades of baby pink – they may be transparent or have an opaque milky finish.

✓ Rose quartz beads make elegant and delicate jewellery.

✓ The beads look good when mixed with silver or other types of semiprecious stones.

✓ Rose quartz beads can also be used as spacers.

✗ They may vary slightly in size and appearance.

◉ Heavy (for larger beads) or medium string, cord, elastic and ribbon.

EXTRAORDINARY TURQUOISE

● *The extraordinary colours of turquoise beads, ranging from sky blue to dark green, open up many different design possibilities.*

● *Large single turquoise beads can make stunning pendants; smaller beads look great set in silver.*

DESIGNING WITH AMBER

● *Amber is an organic material and some of the large, naturally shaped beads work well as pendants or can be used in chunky bracelets.*

● *Amber beads can also be used as spacer beads or mixed with different semiprecious stones, such as turquoise.*

Haematite beads

✓ Haematite is one of the best-known minerals. It is a compound of iron and comes in silver, grey, black, brown or red. Apart from being used for jewellery, the powder form of haematite is used in fabrics and paints.

✓ Haematite, due to its magnetic qualities, is believed to regulate the blood.

✓ Haematite beads make beautiful eveningwear.

✓ They are often used as spacer beads or magnetic clasps.

✓ Haematite beads come in different shapes and sizes and are suitable for almost any type of design.

✗ Haematite can get stuck to other metal objects you are wearing, such as belts, due to its magnetic properties.

✗ It is not suitable for people with pacemakers.

◎ Heavy and medium beading wire, elastic, cord, leather and chain.

Jasper beads

✓ Jasper comes in many colours, usually with striped, flamed or spotted markings. Different types of jasper have specific names, such as agate, Picasso, Egyptian, blue-veined, green, purple, red, zebra and more.

✓ Jasper is believed to bring out special characteristics when worn, for example it may give the wearer courage to speak out.

✓ Jasper can add a traditional or modern look to a design and can be easily mixed with other semiprecious stones.

✗ Larger stones can be quite heavy, so are not suitable for making earrings.

◎ Heavy and medium beading wire, elastic, cord, leather and chain.

BALANCED DESIGN – TIGER-EYE

● *Tiger-eye beads are known for their golden shimmer and look beautiful set in or mixed with silver.*

● *If different sizes of beads are used, it's important to keep a balance by placing the largest bead in the middle – in this case, the doughnut-shaped tiger-eye bead.*

CARVED STONES

● *Semiprecious stones, in this case lapis lazuli and crystal quartz, are quite often carved into unusual decorative objects or pendants.*

● *Carved pendants don't need to be accompanied with other semiprecious beads; they can look beautiful on their own, simply threaded onto chain or another material.*

Peridot beads

✓ Peridot is a sparkling, transparent pale-green stone.

✓ Different shades of peridot beads can be used to make a beautiful and elegant piece of jewellery.

✓ Peridot beads look good set in silver or gold.

✓ Large peridot beads and pendants can be expensive – start with tiny drilled peridot chips to build up your confidence first.

✗ Handle peridot carefully; it scratches easily.

◎ Heavy, medium and light beading wire; elastic, cord, leather and chain.

Green quartz beads

✓ Green quartz belongs to the quartz aventurine family – it comes in many shades of green, from dark to pale, with unique green and black markings.

✓ Green quartz beads and pendants are available in many different shapes and sizes.

✓ Green quartz is very popular in jewellery design because the stone is scratch resistant and can be easily mixed with other semiprecious stones.

✗ Larger beads can be quite heavy, so are not suitable for making earrings.

◎ Heavy, medium and light beading wire; elastic, cord, leather and chain.

REPEAT DESIGN WITH JASPER BEADS

● *Unusual markings and shapes make these jasper beads very special; to show them in their full beauty the same pattern was repeated, and they are divided with small antique silver spacer beads.*

Tiger-eye beads

✓ Tiger-eye is a rock in yellow, honey, red or brown colours with a golden shimmer. It is also known as 'anniversary stone', and is widely used in beads and pendants.

✓ Tiger-eye beads and pendants come in different shapes and sizes. The shimmering, eye-catching texture of the beads can create jewellery suitable for men and women, and for all occasions.

✓ Tiger-eye can be mixed with other types of semiprecious beads, especially those of contrasting colours.

✗ Colours and sizes of handcrafted beads may vary.

◎ Heavy and medium beading wire, elastic, cord, leather and chain.

Lapis lazuli beads

✓ The colour of lapis lazuli is natural deep blue, but it also can be green-blue or purple-blue.

✓ Lapis lazuli beads are often used for men's jewellery.

✓ It can be carved easily.

✓ Lapis lazuli beads can be mixed with other semiprecious beads, but they look stunning on their own, especially when set in silver.

✗ Cheap synthetic lapis lazuli may be mistaken for the real natural stone – however, synthetic lapis is more porous.

◎ Heavy and medium beading wire, elastic, cord, leather and chain.

LAVA AND CRYSTAL QUARTZ

● *Some semiprecious stones are quite heavy and therefore are not suitable for making earrings.*

● *Lava beads are unusual because of their bubbly texture and also because they are very light, and therefore are suitable for chunky jewellery or earrings.*

● *Lava beads come in dark matt colours (black or brown) and look good when mixed with contrasting colours – in this case small crystal quartz chip beads have been added for a little sparkle.*

Lava beads

✓ Lava beads come in shades of dark brown or black and different shapes and sizes.

✓ They are very lightweight and suitable for making chunky designs without worrying about weight.

✓ The bubbly, holey texture gives an unusual look and the lava beads can be easily mixed with different colours.

✗ Since lava beads come from volcanic material, they may need to be cleaned before use.

◎ Light and medium beading wire, cord, leather, ribbon, elastic and chain.

Garnet beads

✓ Garnet comes in many colours, but the most well known is dark red with burgundy tones, looking almost black.

✓ Garnet beads come in a wide range of shapes and sizes and look wonderful mixed with other semiprecious stones in different shades of red.

✓ Because of their deep, wonderful colour, they will add a little bit of drama and glamour to your designs.

✗ Garnet beads are relatively expensive.

◎ Medium and light beading wire, elastic, cord, ribbon and chain.

MIXED SHAPES – HAEMATITE

● *Haematite comes in many shapes and sizes that can be mixed to excellent effect.*

● *Here, geometric, round and butterfly shapes work really well together and little Swarovski crystal beads have been added for sparkle at the end of the butterfly charm.*

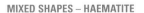

Metal beads

Metal beads are usually used as spacer beads and can add an extra dimension to your designs. They are made out of metals such as aluminium, copper, brass, sterling silver, gold or platinum. Metal beads with holes are made from sheets of metal, which is shaped into a design and soldered together. Small metal beads are cut from metal tubes.

Metal beads come in many different colours, including gold, silver, bronze, copper, brass and antique silver. They can be quite heavy; therefore they will add weight to your design. Some metal beads can have sharp edges around the holes, so it's important to use strong threading materials, such as tigertail wire.

PATTERNED METAL AND RING BEADS

● Mixing different shapes and types of beads can make unique-looking jewellery.
● In this piece, large fabric flower beads have been used as a central point and metal rings threaded onto the chain links emphasize the crystal beads. The large oval and curled patterned beads make a big statement in this design.

METAL BEADS CAN BE FINISHED IN A RANGE OF WAYS:

● Hammering, moulding or stamping patterns/texture into the metal by hand or with a machine.
● Using polishing, brushing and soft granulating machinery to give a smooth or frosted (stardust) finish.
● Filigree – wires are soldered together and formed into patterns.
● Granulation – adding small grains of metal on the top of the bead surface.
● Enamelling – firing a powdered glass onto the metal surface.
● Cloisonné – soldering wires together and forming them into a design and then filling the empty spaces between the wires with enamel.

TUBES AND FROSTED STARDUST BEADS

● Metal beads can be easily mixed with other types of beads, but they look very interesting when combined with each other.
● Here, small dark silver and larger light silver frosted shimmering stardust balls were mixed with tubes for an unusual look.

Hammered and moulded beads

✓ Using different hammers and chisels can add unique patterns, textures and effects to metal.
✓ Patterns can also be moulded or stamped into beads by machine; larger beads of this type can make beautiful pendants.
✓ Hammered, moulded or stamped beads are perfect for many different projects and can also be used as spacers between other styles of beads.
✗ Larger hammered or moulded beads can be quite heavy.
◎ Heavy or medium beading wire, cord, leather, chain and elastic.

Aluminium beads

✓ Aluminium beads are much lighter and cheaper than other metal beads.
✓ Available in a broad range of shapes, colours and sizes.
✓ Aluminium beads can be easily mixed with other metal beads or used as spacers.
✓ Vintage-looking aluminium rose beads come in a variety of colours and sizes and are useful not only for jewellery projects, but also for other craft applications.
✗ Some aluminium beads are quite soft and can be easily damaged if strong pressure is applied.
◎ Medium and light beading wire, soft cord, chain, ribbon and elastic.

Granulated metal beads

✓ Granulating is the process of covering the surface of metal beads with small grains of metal.
✓ These beads come in vibrant patterns (fancy or simple) and they can be easily mixed with other types of beads. They are especially suitable for chunky designs.
✓ Granulated beads can also be used as spacer beads.
✗ There may be slight variations in size and appearance.
◎ Medium and light beading wire, cord, chain, ribbon and elastic.

Enamelled beads and charms

✓ Enamel is a decorative glass coating applied to the metal surface by heat. Enamelled beads and charms come in many colours, shapes and sizes and can be mixed with other types of beads.
✓ Enamelled charms are pretty accessories and can be attached to different projects such as charm bracelets, handbag tassels and bookmarks. Metal charms may also be collectable items.
✗ Enamel painting may be passed off as real enamel; it looks similar but doesn't last as long.
◎ Medium and light beading wire, cord, chain, ribbon and elastic.

Bead facts

Top properties

○ Metal beads are often used as spacers and can give a modern or a vintage look to your design, depending on the beads you choose.
○ Metal charms can be easily attached and reattached to different jewellery projects.
○ Available in a great selection of sizes, shapes and finishes.
○ They are widely available at affordable prices.
○ Can be easily mixed with other types of beads.

Finishes

○ Plain or smooth, decorated/hammered by hand or machine, rough or frosted (stardust), enamelled or granulated, filigree or cloisonné, shiny or tarnished.

Materials

○ Brass, copper, aluminium and other mixtures of base metals.
○ Sterling silver, gold, white gold, platinum and mixtures of precious metals.

Colours

○ Different colours and shades of silver, copper, brass and gold.
○ Enamelled beads come in a huge variety of colours.

Shapes

○ Round and oval, rectangle, triangle, square, tube (curved or straight), barrel, disk, rondelle, ring, heart and many more.

Care

○ Do not spray metal beads with perfume or hairspray as they may tarnish. Clean them with a soft cloth after wearing.
○ Take them off when swimming or bathing.
○ Keep them away from heat and direct sunlight.

Filigree beads

✓ Filigree beads are formed from soldered wire. They come in many different colours, shapes and sizes.
✓ They are very delicate and ornamental.
✓ Filigree beads can add a vintage but fashionable look to your design or may be used as spacers between mixed types of beads.
✓ Many fabulous and high-quality filigree beads come from the Czech Republic, such as filigree combined with Swarovski crystals.
✗ Some filigree beads can be quite expensive, especially ones decorated with Swarovski crystals.
◎ Medium and light beading wire, soft cord, chain, ribbon and elastic.

Smooth and frosted beads

✓ Frosted (stardust) and smooth metal beads are great for mixing with all other beads.
✓ They come in different colours, shapes and sizes and are widely available.
✓ Smooth and frosted metal beads give your design a shimmering and elegant touch.
✓ These beads can be used for different projects, but are used mainly as spacers.
✗ Some bead holes can be quite sharp and may cut soft threading material such as elastic or soft nylon.
◎ Medium and light beading wire, cord, chain and ribbon.

ENAMELLED BEADS

● Enamelled multicoloured beads are fun to work with and can be mixed with other metal beads.
● Designing with Pandora-style colourful enamelled beads is easy and they make really pretty bracelets.

FILIGREE COMBINED WITH RHINESTONE SWAROVSKI BEADS

● Filigree beads combined with rhinestone Swarovski beads give a stunning effect, although they are quite expensive.
● The filigree beads would look beautiful on their own, but in this earring design the red fire-polished drop bead has been added for completeness and balance.

COLOURFUL CLOISONNÉ

● Cloisonné beads are unique and colourful with individual designs.
● These beads threaded onto memory wire make a beautiful bracelet with an oriental look.

Cloisonné beads

✓ Cloisonné beads are made out of soldered wire formed into a shape (similar to the filigree technique), but here the spaces between the wires are filled with enamel.
✓ Cloisonné beads have an oriental look (though they come from all over the world these days).
✓ They come in vibrant colours and individual designs, ideal for making eye-catching jewellery.
✗ Mixing cloisonné beads can be a challenge as they are so unique and very colourful.
◎ Light and medium beading wire, soft cord, leather, ribbon, elastic and chain.

Tube and ring beads

✓ Tubes and rings are often used as spacers. They come in different shapes, sizes and finishes (plain or decorated).
✓ Curved tubes are simple and elegant and space beads evenly.
✓ Metal rings may be plain or decorated, and come in different colours and sizes. They can be used as spacers.
✓ Usually have quite large holes; they are often used in elastic bracelets and chunky jewellery designs.
✗ Large holes in metal rings can be a disadvantage when mixing small and large beads, as small beads may disappear inside the larger beads.
◎ Light and medium beading wire, ribbon, elastic, cord and chain.

Natural beads

Natural beads include shell, horn, bone, seeds, nuts and herbs and spices such as cloves or black pepper. Many of these beads come in natural colours, but some are treated; for example they may be dyed or bleached. Natural beads come in many sizes, shapes and colours and there is a huge range of styles to choose from. They also come in different finishes such as rustic, matt, polished, carved or painted.

Some people are allergic to metal, so natural beads may be ideal for them, though vegetarians may be reluctant to wear horn and bone beads. Bone and horn beads look very similar to ivory, but the selling or export of ivory is illegal in many countries, including the UK and the USA. One of the oldest and most popular natural materials used in bead jewellery is seashell.

SEASHELL BEADS AND PENDANTS

• *Layers of spiral-shaped seashell beads with a beautiful metallic shimmer, threaded on elastic, make a simple but elegant bracelet.*

• *A seashell pendant simply threaded onto leather, suede or cord can make a quick-to-make and effective piece of jewellery.*

Seashell beads

✓ Shells are easy to find on the beach.
✓ Shell beads come in many sizes, shapes and colours and are known for their shimmering effect; they reflect the light beautifully.
✓ Shell beads are lightweight and can be easily mixed with other types of natural beads.
✗ Some types of shell break easily.
◉ Medium or light beading wire, cord, leather, chain, elastic and ribbon.

Decorated and carved seashell pendants

✓ Carved and decorated or hand-painted larger seashells make stunning pendants.
✓ Quick and easy jewellery projects can be made by simply threading handcrafted seashell pendants onto the desired length of cord, leather or ribbon.
✓ All pendants come in different shapes, sizes and colours.
✗ The surface of handcrafted seashells can be easily scratched or damaged.
◉ Medium and light beading wire, soft cord, chain, ribbon and elastic.

Horn and bone beads

✓ Horns and bones are organic materials (like pearls, coral, and amber) that have been used for thousands of years for making jewellery.
✓ They can be easily carved, engraved, shaped, dyed and polished.
✓ Bone beads come mainly from cows and sheep – animals that are killed for their meat. They are legal and affordable, though vegetarians may prefer to avoid them.
✓ Animals shed horns annually, so horn beads may be a good alternative to bone, because the animal need not be killed to obtain them.
✓ Horns can be easily carved, engraved, and drilled.
✗ Horns and bones can easily stain.
✗ Ivory is illegal and should not be used.
✗ All horns and bones require care to keep them in top condition: shop them in jewellery boxes or soft pouches, and keep them away from perfumes, hairspray, water and extreme temperatures.
◉ Medium and light beading wire, cord, leather, suede, ribbon and elastic.

BONES COMBINED WITH SEMIPRECIOUS STONES

• *An easy way to dye bone beads is to soak them in coffee or tea for a few hours. The longer they are soaked, the darker they'll get.*

• *This elastic bracelet is made out of a combination of turquoise, metal and natural and dyed double-hole bone beads. The turquoise stones, with their contrasting colour, emphasize the colour of the bones – silver metal beads keep the piece unified.*

DESIGNING WITH SPICES

• *Star anise is widely used in Chinese cooking. However, this beautiful star-shaped spice can also be used as a decorative object or bead.*

• *Thread star anise and peppercorns onto thin but strong thread. Use a heavy-duty needle for making holes through the spices.*

• *Apply clear nail polish for a glossy finish.*

Bead facts

Top properties
○ Some natural 'beads' can be found easily, such as shells from the beach, or seeds and nuts.
○ Natural beads can be easily treated, drilled, pierced, carved, engraved and decorated.
○ They can be effectively mixed with other types of natural beads.

○ Natural beads make unusual and affordable jewellery designs.
○ Natural beads come in many colours, shapes, sizes and finishes.

Finishes
○ Natural, dyed, painted, engraved, carved, varnished or polished.

Materials
○ Nuts, seeds, spices, shell, bone, horn and ivory.

Colours
○ Many different colours, but mainly white, reds, blues and browns.

Shapes
○ Natural beads come in a range of regular and irregular shapes and sizes – or may be carved into a particular style.

Care
○ To keep natural beads in top condition, shop them in jewellery boxes or soft pouches.

○ Wipe them with a soft cloth after use.
○ Take them off when swimming, bathing or going to the sauna.
○ Keep them away from heat, perfumes and hairspray.

Seed beads

✓ You can make seed beads from all kinds of items that you might usually throw away, such as fruit and vegetable seeds, beans or tree seeds (pinecones). Keep the seeds and, while they are wet, make a hole through them with a heavy-duty needle or awl. Let them dry naturally on a paper towel.

✓ Making your own seed beads is an inexpensive or even free way of expanding your existing bead collection.

✓ Seed beads make very unique jewellery; they come in a wide variety of sizes and shapes and can be mixed together to great effect.

✓ Seed beads may be used in their natural form or treated in different ways such as dyeing, painting, bleaching or polishing.

✗ Some seed beads break if strong pressure is applied.

◎ Medium and light beading wire, natural cord, elastic.

Spice beads

✓ Many spices can be used for beads in their natural form – such as different types of pepper, cloves, cinnamon and many more.

✓ Dried spices can be pierced with a heavy-duty needle and threaded onto natural threads or cords.

✓ It's possible to apply different finishes to spice beads by polishing, varnishing (ordinary nail polish can be used) or painting them.

✗ Some spice beads have a very strong aroma, which some people may find too strong.

◎ Medium and light beading wire, natural cord and elastic.

Nut beads

✓ Nuts are natural products and once dried they become very hard, almost like wood. Then holes can be drilled through the nuts and they can be treated in different ways such as being dyed, painted, varnished, polished or just used in their natural form.

✓ Nuts can be carved just like any other material.

✓ Beautiful nuts with very attractive markings come from palm trees in different parts of the world; try coconut, betel and buri.

✓ Fascinating combinations of nuts can make unusual jewellery pieces.

✗ The shape and size of nuts can be irregular.

◎ Medium and light beading wire, natural cord and elastic.

SEED BEADS
○ A cheap jewellery solution!
○ Beans come in different colours, shapes and sizes, so are ideal for all kinds of jewellery designs. Soak beans in water until they get soft then, using a heavy-duty needle, thread them onto thin but strong threading material.
○ The threading material, for example hemp, may be visible and a part of the design. Bean beads look good combined with wooden beads or any other natural beads.

NUTS MIXED WITH BEADS
○ Coconut shells can be treated, carved and decorated for use in jewellery.
○ Nut beads may be mixed with other natural beads such as wood or seeds, or with other types of beads such as glass.
○ Due to their natural look, these materials look better when threaded onto natural cotton cords or hemp.

Plastic and acrylic beads

In the past the plastic beads were considered cheap and not of very good quality. You can still find beads like these, but today plastic and acrylic beads are often so well made that it can be hard to tell the difference between them and the material they are imitating.

Plastic and acrylic beads can be made to simulate glass, metal or even semiprecious beads – sometimes you need to touch them to tell them apart from the real thing; these other materials are much cooler to the touch and heavier than plastic beads. Plastic beaded jewellery is easy to wear and, because it is lightweight, plastic is often used to make items for children. Plastic and acrylic beads come in an enormous variety of colours, sizes, shapes and finishes. They are reasonably priced and can be easily mixed with other types of beads.

FUNKY CHILDREN'S PLASTIC BEADS

- *Children's plastic beads usually come in bright, beautiful colours with big holes for easy threading.*
- *These beads are cleverly designed to interlink with each other for a funky look. Simply thread the beads randomly onto an elastic thread for a stunning bracelet.*

IMITATION STONE

- *Plastic beads imitating stones come in many styles, colours and shapes.*
- *These beads are usually large but very light; therefore they can be used comfortably as pendants.*

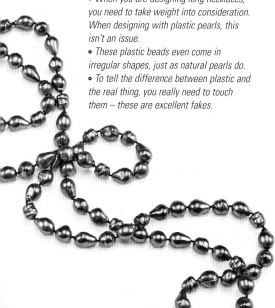

LONG NECKLACE IN PLASTIC PEARLS

- *When you are designing long necklaces, you need to take weight into consideration. When designing with plastic pearls, this isn't an issue.*
- *These plastic beads even come in irregular shapes, just as natural pearls do.*
- *To tell the difference between plastic and the real thing, you really need to touch them – these are excellent fakes.*

Children's beads

✓ Children's plastic beads come in many bright colours, and different shapes and sizes.

✓ They have big holes, so they are easy to thread onto any material, usually elastic.

✓ Some children's beads are designed in such a way that they are easily interlinked, creating a particular effect.

✓ Alphabet beads can be used to create personalized pieces such as keyrings or bag charms.

✗ Beads are not suitable for children under three years old, as they are a choking hazard.

◉ Medium or light beading wire, cord, leather, chain, elastic and ribbon.

Patterned beads

✓ Patterned plastic or acrylic beads come in many different sizes, shapes, colours and effects such as marble, wood, stone, glass, metallic, satin, antique, ceramic, faceted, leopard skin, checkered, dotted, stripy, simulated lampwork and many more.

✓ High-quality material is used for making these beads.

✓ Faceted plastic beads don't reflect as much light as real crystal beads, but they make a good low-cost substitute.

✗ The bead surface can be easily scratched or damaged.

◉ Medium and light beading wire, cord, ribbon, suede cord and elastic.

Plastic pearls

✓ Plastic pearls are widely used for making fashion jewellery and they come in many different sizes, colours and finishes, such as smooth, shiny, frosted and metallic.

✓ Good-quality pearl imitations are also called faux pearls, and may be made out of different materials such as glass and shells. You can test the difference between natural pearls and faux pearls with your teeth. Rub a pearl against your teeth – real pearl will feel gritty while faux will feel smooth.

✗ Keep plastic pearls away from heat, as plastic is heat-formed.

◉ Medium and light beading wire, soft cord, chain, ribbon and elastic.

Lucite beads

✓ Lucite is a good-quality lightweight and low-cost plastic that was popular in the 1950s and 1960s for making jewellery, as well as fashionable shoe heels.

✓ Original Lucite beads can be collectable.

✓ Many Lucite beads are shaped into flowers or leaves but other shapes are also available.

✓ Lucite beads are very finely finished and are suitable for costume jewellery or vintage designs.

✗ Genuine vintage Lucite beads are hard to find.

◉ Medium and light beading wire, cord, ribbon, suede cord and elastic.

The facts

Top properties

∘ Plastic and acrylic beads are widely available, inexpensive and lightweight.

∘ They come in a variety of colours, shapes, sizes and finishes.

∘ They can imitate other types of beads, such as metal or stone, for a fraction of the price.

∘ Plastic and acrylic beads are suitable for children's as well as adults' projects and they are easy to mix with other types of beads.

∘ Plastic and acrylic beads can be used in a range of crafts other than jewellery making.

Finishes

∘ Transparent, translucent, opaque, metallic, stone, wood, glass, satin.

Materials

∘ Plastic, acrylic, resin and Lucite.

Colours

∘ Many different colours and effects are available – rainbow colours are very popular for children's plastic beads.

Shapes

∘ Many different shapes available, including round, oval, barrel, drop, star, cube, heart, flower, leaf and many more.

Care

∘ To keep plastic beads in good condition, store them in jewellery boxes or soft pouches.

∘ Wipe them with a soft cloth to clear dust or with damp cloth to remove dirt.

∘ Take them off when swimming, bathing or going to a sauna.

∘ Keep them away from heat.

∘ Do not clean them with any sharp objects as they scratch easily.

Silver acrylic beads

✓ Acrylic is a plastic substance that is used in various products such as paint, fake fingernails, fabrics, furniture and jewellery.

✓ Silver acrylic beads are an inexpensive way of adding another texture to jewellery designs without adding any more weight. They are often used as spacer beads.

✓ Silver acrylic beads come in many different shapes and sparkling finishes.

✓ Large silver acrylic beads make beautiful pendants.

✗ These beads will break if not handled carefully.

◎ Medium and light beading wire, cord, ribbon and elastic.

Stone imitation beads

✓ Plastic and acrylic beads come in imitation stone finishes such as turquoise, jasper and many more.

✓ The price is the first difference between real and imitation stone. Some plastic and acrylic imitations are such good quality it is hard to tell the difference between them and the real thing.

✓ As well as being cheap and light, plastic and acrylic imitation stone beads come in many shapes and colours, offering a huge choice.

✗ The bead surface can be easily scratched or damaged if not handled properly.

◎ Medium and light beading wire, cord, ribbon, suede cord and elastic.

METALLIC-FINISH ACRYLIC BEADS

∘ Mixing acrylic beads with different metallic finishes can make for a modern and sophisticated-looking piece of jewellery.

∘ The silver acrylic beads complement and emphasize the bronze acrylic beads – don't be afraid to mix different metallic finishes together.

Laminated resin beads

✓ Resin is a type of plastic that can be easily moulded.

✓ Resin beads are inexpensive and come in a wide range of colours, shapes and sizes, and they don't fade.

✓ Laminated beads are made of resin sheets joined in colourful layers, which are then formed into the bead.

✓ They are bright and cheerful and are suitable for designing jewellery to match summer outfits. They are especially good for simple elastic bracelet designs.

✗ Resin beads are easy to scratch.

◎ Medium or light beading wire, cord, chain or elastic.

Glass-effect beads

✓ Plastic glass-effect beads come in many colours, sizes, shapes (oval, round, tube) and finishes (transparent, translucent, opaque, faceted).

✓ It can be hard to tell the difference between these and real glass.

✓ These beads are lighter than real glass beads, so are useful for making a piece less heavy.

✗ These beads will show scratches.

◎ Medium or light beading wire, cord, chain and elastic.

SILVER AND COLOURED ACRYLIC BEADS

∘ Silver acrylic beads look like metal, but they are much lighter and cheaper.

∘ Silver acrylic ball beads and colourful flower beads threaded onto memory wire can create a beautiful bracelet. Memory wire bracelets do not need a clasp and they are easy to put on your wrist.

Crystal beads

Natural crystals are known as 'rock crystal' and they belong to the semiprecious stone family. The crystals shown here are lead glass that is formed into crystal. Lead is an important element in turning glass into crystal. It is heavier than glass, and makes cutting easier and the crystals sparkle.

The quality and price of crystal beads depends on the lead content. For example, Swarovski crystal contains a much higher percentage of lead than other crystal beads and therefore is considered the best-quality crystal in the world. The look of each bead also depends on the way that the crystal is cut. 'Faceted cut' is a cutting technique where the edge of the glass is cut flat. The light travels from one angle (facet) to another, creating a spectrum of colours. Each cut can have a different number of facets, which will form the shape of the crystal. Different cuts have names such as 'single', 'full', 'hexagon' and 'cabochon'.

MIXED CRYSTALS AND BEADS

• *Faceted Swarovski bicone crystals are easy to mix with other types of beads, such as small glass seed beads or Swarovski pearls.*

• *For a vintage look, use antique silver spacers and chains.*

SMALL FACETED DROPS

• *This drop earring design is timeless – faceted crystal drops are ideal for this piece.*

• *Drop earrings with faceted crystals will reflect the light with every movement and sparkle beautifully.*

Faceted Swarovski bicone beads with AB coating

✓ Bicone Swarovski faceted beads (with AB coating) reflect light beautifully; this effect makes them the first choice for many jewellery makers and designers.

✓ The beads come in different colours and sizes.

✓ Traditionally, Swarovski beads have been used for making wedding jewellery and accessorizing wedding dresses, but today they come in many modern shapes.

✓ You can easily mix Swarovski faceted bicone beads with other types of beads – in fact, some designs look much better with only a few crystals.

✗ Some Swarovski crystals are expensive.

◎ Medium or light beading wire, cord, leather, chain, elastic and ribbon.

Crystal pendants

✓ Crystal pendants come in different colours and sizes, with or without AB coating.

✓ They also come in many shapes such as heart, flower, cross, leaf, pear, drop, butterfly and many more.

✓ Crystal pendants can be simply threaded onto cord, leather or silk as a focal point for a quick and stunning jewellery project.

✗ If you are using a metal pendant holder, make sure that you secure it properly, as heavy crystal pendants can easily slip out.

◎ Heavy, medium or light beading wire, cord, ribbon, leather, chain and elastic.

Swarovski bicone beads

✓ Swarovski bicone beads without AB coating can be just as beautiful as the coated variety.

✓ These beads come in different colours and sizes with high-quality finishes.

✓ Many glamorous jewellery designs can be created with Swarovski beads.

✗ Many fake Swarovski beads are available, so make sure that you are buying the genuine articles.

◎ Medium and light beading wire, soft cord, chain, ribbon and elastic.

Hot-fix crystal flat backs

✓ Hot-fix crystal flat backs are used for brightening clothes, shoes and accessories.

✓ Hot-fix crystals have pre-applied heat-sensitive glue on their backs, which melts with heat and forms a bond with fabric or other material.

✓ You need to use an appropriate tool to apply hot-fix crystals, such as a touch hot-fix applicator – follow the manufacturer's instructions for use carefully.

✗ Hot-fix crystals can get stuck in the applicator.

◎ Hot-fix crystals will stick to most materials, except for smooth leather.

The facts

Top properties
○ Crystal beads will add glamour and sparkle to your designs.
○ They come in a variety of sizes colours, shapes and finishes.
○ These beads are widely available in different price ranges. The higher-quality ones, such as Swarovski crystal, are more expensive.

○ Crystals can be easily mixed with other beads.
○ Crystals can make stunning pendants.

Finishes
○ Faceted (fire-polished), unfaceted, with or without coating (AB).

Materials
○ Glass and lead.

Colours
○ Many colours are available and there are also charts to help you make your choice.

Shapes
○ Many different shapes are available such as round, oval, barrel, drop, rondelle, disc, star, cube, heart, flower and leaf – the most common is the bicone shape.

Care
○ To keep crystals in top condition, store them in a box or a soft pouch.
○ Use a soft cloth with gentle pressure to clean; if necessary rinse in warm water. Make sure that they are dried properly before you store them again.
○ Take crystal beads off when swimming or bathing.
○ Don't use sharp objects to clean them as they scratch easily.

Faceted rondelle beads
✓ The Czech Republic is known for making high-quality faceted glass beads – they use the term 'fire polished'.
✓ Faceted crystal rondelles come in many colours and sizes and they are easy to mix with other types of beads.
✗ Make sure that you use strong beading wire if you are going to use a lot of rondelle beads in your project (for example a fully beaded bracelet) because these beads add a lot of weight to a design.
◎ Medium and light beading wire, cord, ribbon and elastic.

Faceted twisted coin beads
✓ Faceted twisted coin beads sparkle from many different angles due to their cut and shape.
✓ These beads can be used as pendants or charms.
✓ They come in many beautiful colours, ranging from clear to smoky dark grey.
✗ Because of their weight, these beads are not suitable for making long, dangling earrings.
◎ Medium and light beading wire, cord, ribbon, suede cord and elastic.

RIBBON AND FACETED RONDELLE CRYSTALS
○ Rondelle crystals can easily rub against each other. Prevent that by using ribbon (in a contrasting or a matching colour) as a threading material, making knots between each bead. This will soften the look of the beads and act as part of the design. Using a few metal spacer beads and other components can add extra texture and enhance volume.

Fine hexagon-cut faceted beads
✓ The degree of sparkle of these crystal beads depends on the number and shape of the facets.
✓ Many tiny hexagon-shaped facets really sparkle in the light and look gorgeous in any colour.
✓ Large, fine-cut hexagon beads make stunning pendants.
✓ Fine hexagon-cut crystal beads are easy to mix with different types of beads.
✗ Larger beads can make a noise when they rub against each other (using spacer beads or knots can prevent this).
◎ Heavy or medium beading wire, cord, leather, chain and elastic.

Hexagon-cut faceted beads
✓ A striking faceted hexagon cut gives beads a unique sparkling look.
✓ Faceted hexagon-cut beads come in different sizes and colours.
✓ Faceted hexagon-cut beads can be used in a variety of jewellery designs and are easy to mix with other types of beads.
✗ Faceted hexagon-cut beads are easily scratched.
◎ Heavy or medium beading wire, cord, leather, chain and elastic.

LARGE CRYSTAL DROP PENDANT

● *Large crystal drops make beautiful pendants. Sparkling pendants look stunning simply threaded onto a length of leather.*

● *This could be worn as a daytime casual piece of jewellery, or as eveningwear.*

Faceted cube beads

✓ Faceted cube beads can have a hole drilled from the middle of one side to another side or a hole running from corner to corner (called a diagonal cube).

✓ Faceted cubes give jewellery designs an unusual geometric look.

✓ Faceted cubes can be easily mixed with other types of beads; they can also be used as spacer beads.

✗ Diagonal cubes will have points sticking out when they are threaded – keep that in mind when designing.

◉ Medium or light beading wire, cord, chain and elastic.

Faceted crystal drop beads

✓ Faceted crystal drop beads come in a variety of colours and sizes.

✓ Larger crystal drops will add glamour to your designs and can be used as pendants or central focal points.

✓ Smaller crystal drops are ideal for making earrings.

✗ Large crystal drop beads are quite heavy, and are not suitable for earrings.

◉ Medium or light beading wire, cord, chain and elastic.

Opal faceted crystals

✓ Opal faceted crystal beads can be just as beautiful as the translucent kind.

✓ Opal crystal beads are less glitzy and more subtle than the translucent ones so may be more suited to day wear.

✓ Opal crystals can be easily mixed with other types of beads; they can also be used as spacer beads.

✗ The greater opacity of these beads lowers their brilliance because not as much light is transmitted through the beads. However they are still reflective.

✗ Available in fewer colours than the translucent beads.

◉ Medium or light beading wire, cord, chain and elastic.

Rectangle-cut round

✓ A modern cut, rectangle-cut rounds have more pointed ends than other rounds.

✓ The simpler cut gives them a more chunky appearance than other crystal cuts.

✓ The rectangle cut provides a large reflective surface in the centre of the beads and gives a geometric look to jewellery.

✗ They are more angular than other bead cuts; this will need to be taken into account when designing.

◉ Medium or light beading wire, cord, chain and elastic.

SHAPED CRYSTAL BEADS

● *Faceted crystal hearts and flowers dangle from this necklace.*

● *Crystal bicones and round glass beads interspersed by metal spacers provide a setting for the eye-catching dangles.*

● *A warm colour scheme of reds and purples really leaps out.*

Opaque faceted crystals

✓ Opaque faceted crystal beads are available in many shapes, just as the translucent crystals are.

✓ Opaque crystal beads are ideal for smart eveningwear because they are reflective but not translucent.

✓ Opaque crystals can be easily mixed with other types of beads; they can also be used as spacer beads.

✗ The greater opacity of these beads means they tend to be slightly muted in colour.

✗ Available in fewer colours than the translucent beads.

◎ Medium or light beading wire, cord, chain and elastic.

Faceted crystal shapes

✓ Faceted crystal beads in alternative shapes, such as flowers and hearts.

✓ In the case of the hearts the holes are drilled through the top so they can be used like drop beads, or with a bail for a pendant.

✓ The crystal flowers are drilled through the centre and would work well as spacers.

✗ Greater consideration needs to be given to the position of the hole than for other bead shapes.

◎ Medium or light beading wire, cord, chain and elastic.

CRYSTAL AND PEARL TIARA

• *Wedding jewellery often includes pearls and crystals – they look fabulous together.*

• *A simple and elegant bridal headband/tiara can be made with pearls and round, faceted hexagon crystal beads, using the wire wrapping technique (see page 130).*

CRYSTAL BEAD COLOUR CHART

• *Crystal bead colour charts are a quick way for you to find the colour and finish of crystal bead that you need for your design. They are numbered, have a sample of the bead attached and sometimes its name. You can use the number to order exactly what you need from the manufacturer or supplier. Different manufacturers do have different colour numbering systems.*

Code		Code		Code	
401		421		441	
402		422		442	
403		423		443	
404		424		444	
405		425		445	
406		426		446	
407		427		447	
408		428		448	
409		429		449	
410		430		450	
411		431		451	
412		432		452	
413		433		453	
414		434		454	
415		435		455	
416		436		456	
417		437		457	
418		438		458	
419		439		459	
420		440		460	

Fabric-covered beads

Beads can be covered with different fabrics; this is easy to do yourself at home. You can also use this technique to revive old and faded beads that you don't like any more. Many ready-made fabric beads are available to buy and they come in different colours, shapes and sizes for a reasonable price.

Felted wool beads are fun for jewellery making, and are a great project for making use of that woolly jumper that shrank a few days ago in the wash. Handwoven knot beads, also known as

Chinese ball knots, can be made out of hemp or other cords. Chinese balls are multifunctional, as they can be used as beads or spacers, but also as cufflinks or buttons.

CHINESE BALL KNOT KEYRING
- Key rings decorated with Chinese knots are a quick and easy project that can be used every day. The size of the Chinese knot depends on the size of the cord that they are made from.

Fabric-decorated beads
✓ Fabric beads come in different sizes (usually fairly large), colours and shapes.
✓ Fabric beads can be made easily at home, using all kinds of fabrics.
✓ Decorating your old beads by wrapping fabric around them is a good way of using up fabric scraps and giving your old beads a makeover at the same time.
✓ You can stuff fabric beads with different materials such as old fabrics and wool when they are made from scratch.
✓ Fabric beads can be easily mixed with other beads.
✗ It's hard to clean fabric beads.
◉ Medium or light beading wire, cord, leather, chain, elastic and ribbon.

Chinese ball knots
✓ Chinese ball knots (also known as handwoven knots) come in different colours and sizes and have good-sized holes. The size of the ball will depend on the thickness of the cord.
✓ Chinese ball knots will add a different texture to your jewellery designs.
✓ Chinese ball knots can also be used as spacer beads, bracelets, charms or cufflinks.
✗ Chinese ball knots can easily become dirty.
◉ Medium and light beading wire, cord, ribbon, chain and elastic.

FELT BEADS
- *You don't need to use lots of beads to create a beautiful choker, but you can still follow a few simple design rules.*
- *For instance, use an odd number of beads (one, three, five and so on) for visual balance.*
- *Mixing plain and embellished beads, as here, will make a very pretty choker.*

Fabric beads with metallic effect
✓ The shiny material gives added depth to your design. Metallic effect can be added to fabric in a range of ways.
✓ Fabric beads are easy to thread as they come with large holes.
✗ Glue can damage the surface of your beads or fabrics if not applied properly.
◉ Medium and light beading wire, cord, chain, ribbon and elastic.

Fabric flower-decorated beads
✓ As well as decorating beads with fabrics, you can also use flowers made out of fabric or ribbons.
✓ Simply glue ribbons and flowers onto your beads; for a more textured effect, try adding netting or extra beads.
✓ You can create truly unique-looking beads in this way.
✗ Use an appropriate glue or glue gun to attach other objects securely.
◉ Medium or light beading wire, cord, ribbon, leather, chain and elastic.

The facts

Top properties
○ Fabric beads are easy to make at home.
○ They come in a variety of colours, shapes and sizes.
○ They are widely available and reasonably priced.
○ These beads can add a unique look to your jewellery, especially if you've made them yourself.

○ Fabric beads can also be used as decorative objects.

Finishes
○ Fluffy, fabric, shiny or matt, metallic, plain or embroidered.

Materials
○ Different types of fabrics, yarns, cords and ribbons.

Colours
○ An infinite variety of colours and shades.

Shapes
○ The most common shape is a ball but many other shapes are possible.

Care
○ Store fabric jewellery in a jewellery box or soft pouch.

○ Avoid pressure on felt beads or they will deform.
○ Take fabric beads off when swimming, bathing, cleaning or gardening.
○ Use sticky tape to remove unwanted fluff or dirt from fabric beads.

Fluffy synthetic beads

✓ Fluffy synthetic beads are fun to work with – they are soft to the touch and come in different colours, sizes and shapes such as oval, round and heart.

✓ Fluffy synthetic beads are very light and are easy to mix with other types of beads.

✓ Jewellery made out of fluffy beads is easy to wear because they are so lightweight. They are ideal for making earrings.

✗ Some of the bead holes may be blocked due to the fluffiness, but this can be easily fixed with a bead reamer.

◎ Medium and light beading wire, cord, ribbon, chain and elastic.

Plain and embroidered felt beads

✓ Felt beads are easy to make – all you need is wool, soap and hot water.

✓ Felt beads come in different colours, shapes and sizes and may be plain or embroidered.

✓ Both plain and embroidered beads look fantastic; they are also soft to the touch and very light.

✓ Felt beads can be used for modern or traditional jewellery designs.

✓ They are also popular for other craft projects such as embellishing clothes or bags.

✗ Strong pressure can deform these beads.

◎ Medium or light beading wire, cord, ribbon, leather, chain and elastic.

SOFT-TOUCH FLUFFY EARRINGS
● Fluffy beads are soft to the touch and come in different colours, sizes and shapes.
● Fluffy beads are very light and are easy to mix with other types of beads.

MIXED FABRIC AND METAL BEADS
● Mixing fabric and metal beads can add texture to your jewellery project.
● Gold metal spacer beads emphasize the gold-striped fabric used for the large beads.

FABRIC BEAD NECKLACE
● Large fabric beads are perfect for long necklaces because they are lightweight.
● To emphasize these beads in a design, thread them onto a ribbon, making a knot between each bead.

Seed beads

Seed beads are uniformly shaped beads made by cutting a long glass tube into small pieces. Seed beads come in different colours and finishes (transparent, translucent, opaque, metallic, silver-lined, pearlescent), shapes (cylinder, tube, bugle, plain round, hexagon, cube, drop) and sizes (see chart on page 137).

MIXED BEAD RING
- *This eye-catching 'bling' ring is made out of long, faceted bugle beads mixed with hexagon-faceted beads and crystals.*
- *The length of the bugle beads dictates the form of the finished design.*

Seed beads are sold by size and this can sometimes be confusing, as smaller numbers mean bigger sizes – for example, a size 10 seed bead is bigger than size 12. Seed beads are sold in tubes, on strands or by weight. The quality of seed beads depends on the manufacturer. Japanese and Czech beads are considered the best quality. Seed beads are mostly used in bead-weaving or loomwork. The most common thread used for these techniques is called 'Nymo', and you can buy it in a range of colours and thicknesses.

Seed beads
✓ These are the most common beads and they come in many different colours, sizes and finishes.
✓ The most-used seed bead sizes are between 11 and 6, but this depends on the project.
✓ Seed beads can be used for decorative purposes – they may be attached to paper, furniture or clothes.
✓ Seed beads are widely used for bead-weaving and loomwork techniques.
✓ They can be easily mixed with other types of beads.
✗ Seed beads are very tiny – use adequate lighting to avoid straining your eyes.
◎ Medium or light beading wire, memory wire, elastic and Nymo thread.

Colour-lined seed beads
✓ The colour coating is applied from the inside of the bead, reflecting light and giving the beads an unusual look.
✓ Colour-lined seed beads come in many different colours, sizes and finishes.
✓ Colour-lined seed beads stand out well in a design.
✓ They easily mix with all other types of beads.
✗ Too many thread passes through the hole can cause the lining to wear off.
◎ Medium or light beading wire, memory wire, elastic and Nymo thread.

MULTISTRAND SEED BEAD NECKLACE
- *Working with tiny seed beads is a fussy process but the final outcome can be delightful.*
- *Three colours of beads (blue, brown and white) have been threaded in a random pattern for an interesting and unique look.*
- *Make the clasp out of seed beads for a nontraditional, but subtle, finish.*

Hex seed beads
✓ Hex beads are similar to cylinder beads but they have a hexagon-shaped profile.
✓ The hexagon cut gives these beads extra sparkle.
✓ Hex beads come in different colours, sizes and finishes such as amber, metallic, chocolate, rainbow and haematite.
✓ Hex beads are suitable for all kinds of projects; they can give a vintage look to a design.
✗ Some of the best-quality hex beads come from Japan and these can be quite expensive.
◎ Medium or light beading wire, thin ribbon, soft cord, Nymo thread and elastic.

Drop seed beads
✓ Drop (teardrop shape), dagger (spear shape) and fringe seed beads are all suitable for the edges of beadwork.
✓ Drop seed beads add body and texture to projects.
✓ Drop seed beads come in different colours and sizes.
✓ They can also be used as spacer beads.
✗ Drop, fringe or dagger beads with spiky ends are easily chipped.
◎ Medium or light beading wire, thin ribbon, soft cord, Nymo thread and elastic.

The facts

Top properties
○ Seed beads are perfect for bead-weaving and loomwork projects.
○ Many different types of seed beads are widely available.
○ They can add an extra texture to your jewellery projects and can also be used as spacers.
○ They are easy to mix with other types of beads.
○ Seed beads can be used in many other craft projects, such as embellishing clothes or decorating objects.

Finishes
○ Transparent, translucent, opaque, matt, glossy, metallic, fire-polished (faceted), silver-lined, pearlescent and more.

Materials
○ Most high-quality seed beads are made of glass, but other materials can also be used such as shell, wood, metal and acrylic.

Colours
○ Available in a huge variety of beautiful colours.

Shapes
○ The most common shapes are round, cylinder, hexagon, square (cube), tube (bugle) and teardrop (drop, dagger and fringe).

Care
○ Seed beads are so tiny, it's important to store them properly. Try plastic tubes, bags, flip-top boxes, organizers, storage rings or storage jars.
○ Keep finished pieces in jewellery boxes or soft pouches.
○ Take seed-bead jewellery off when swimming, bathing, cleaning or gardening.
○ Built-up dust or dirt can be removed by washing seed-bead jewellery with soapy water. Rinse and let it dry naturally.

Bugle seed beads
✓ Bugle beads are long, hollow glass tubes cut to length.
✓ They are great for dangling earrings or 'bling' rings.
✓ Bugle beads may be straight or twisted and they come in many different colours and sizes.
✓ They are suitable for the brick-stitch technique in bead-weaving.
✗ Bugle beads usually have sharp edges; keep that in mind when designing.
◎ Medium or light beading wire, memory wire, elastic and Nymo thread.

Cylinder seed beads
✓ Cylinder beads are short tubes with large holes and flat sides.
✓ Cylinder beads have even sizes and fit nicely together – they are good for precision work. Toho and Delica are well-known, high-quality Japanese cylinder bead brands – they have large holes and thin walls.
✓ Cylinder beads come in a range of different colours and can be mixed with many other types of beads.
✗ Japanese cylinder beads can be quite expensive.
◎ Medium and light beading wire, cord, ribbon, chain and elastic.

CUBE BEAD BRACELET
○ Cubes give your project an unusual geometrical look – they are easy to thread as they come with large holes.
○ Cubes can be threaded randomly or in an ordered pattern.

Cube seed beads
✓ Cube seed beads are small, square, smooth beads; they come in many different colours and beautiful finishes.
✓ Cube beads are a high-quality type of seed bead and they are cut in a very precise way.
✓ Because of their uniform look, cube beads are perfect for bead-weaving and can also be used as spacers.
✓ Cube beads look stunning on bracelets but are suitable for all types of designs.
✗ Cheaper cube seed beads might vary in shape and size and won't be as close fitting as the expensive ones. Czech and Japanese are the best-quality seed beads.
◎ Medium or light beading wire, thin ribbon, soft cord, Nymo thread and elastic.

MIXING SHAPES – DROPS AND SEED BEADS
○ Beautiful teardrop-shaped earrings were made out of hex and drop seed beads.
○ Drop-shaped seed beads add extra texture to the design.
○ Hex beads add sparkle and length to the earrings.

NETTED CHOKER
○ A netted choker made with large seed (size 6) beads looks glamorous and elegant, but this technique requires much concentration and counting.

Other beads

Have you ever lost one of your earrings or ended up with a few pieces of broken jewellery? These bits and pieces can be reused for new jewellery projects. For example, unmatched earrings can become charms on bracelets; a broken chain can be cut into smaller pieces and used for dangling earrings.

Ask your friends to give you their broken jewellery if they don't want to keep it. One person's trash is another person's treasure! Beads can also be made out of other easily obtainable household materials, such as aluminium foil or paper, and many everyday objects can be transformed into jewellery – curtain rings, buttons, sequins, tassels… the list is endless. All of these objects can be further decorated with paint, varnish or glued-on embellishments. Let your imagination run riot, and you could end up with totally unique pieces of jewellery.

VINTAGE PAPER FLOWER EARRINGS
- *You can make your own paper flowers or buy them at any craft store.*
- *Pull paper flowers through the middle of the large flower-shaped Lucite beads, make a loop and attach the beads to earring hooks. The paper flowers give these earrings a fantastic vintage look.*

TASSEL PENDANT
- *Maybe you have a few spare curtain rings and tassels lying around? Instead of throwing them away, make a beautiful pendant out of them.*
- *First customize the curtain ring with chain, using a glue gun to attach it. Attach the tassel to the chain and the pendant is ready.*
- *Thread the pendant onto a length of leather to complete this modern-looking piece of jewellery.*

Buttons

✓ Why not use buttons as beads?
✓ Buttons are made from many different materials such as metal, wood or acrylic and they come in different colours, shapes and sizes.
✓ Many different finishes such as metallic, carved or painted, as well as stone-set and fabric-decorated.
✓ Some vintage buttons are custom-made.
✓ Craft buttons are widely available, but why not just raid your sewing box or check for buttons on unwanted items of clothing?
✓ Buttons can make stunning and unusual jewellery.
✗ Some metal buttons can be quite heavy.
◉ Heavy, medium or light beading wire, leather, cord, elastic and ribbon.

Sequins

✓ Sequins are known for their shimmering effect and are used for accessorizing designs by sewing them onto fabric, purses or items of clothing, or for home furnishings such as pillows and lampshades.
✓ The disc is the most common sequin shape, but they are available in many other shapes, as well as different sizes and colours.
✓ Sequins can be threaded onto elastic to make an unusual bracelet.
✗ Making jewellery out of sequins can take a long time, as they are very thin and slippery.
◉ Medium or light beading wire, thin ribbon, soft cord and elastic.

Paper

✓ Lightweight and eco-friendly beads can be made out of recycled paper.
✓ Classic paper beads are made by rolling a strip of paper around knitting needles or straws. The bead must be rolled tightly to avoid spaces between the layers.
✓ Decorative paper flowers are easy to make; these are mainly used for decorating wedding or dinner tables.
✓ Paper flowers can be used to decorate jewellery or beads and add a beautiful vintage look to jewellery.
✗ Paper beads are not water-resistant.
◉ Medium and light beading wire, thin ribbon, soft cord, Nymo thread and elastic.

Wire

✓ Wire is widely used in jewellery projects for making earring hooks, clasps and findings; however, wire can also be used for making beads.
✓ You can make your own wire beads or purchase them from bead stores.
✓ Wire beads come in silver, gold, bronze, copper and black, and in different shapes including round and cube.
✗ When making wire beads at home, ensure that you don't leave any sharp ends of wire sticking out, as they may scratch the wearer or snag clothing.
◉ Medium or light beading wire, memory wire, chain, cord and leather.

The facts

Top properties
◦ Unusual-looking beads can be made at home.
◦ Reuse of old materials for new projects.
◦ An inexpensive way of making beads and jewellery.
◦ These materials are easy to mix with other beads.
◦ They can be used in many other craft projects, such as to embellish clothes or decorate objects.

Finishes
◦ Smooth or rough, matt or shiny, metallic.

Materials
◦ Metal, paper, wood, fabric, foil, wire, glass and plastic.

Colours
◦ Infinite range of colours.

Shapes
◦ Round, oval, disc, flower, ring and many more.

Care
◦ Paper beads are not water-resistant.
◦ Light beads, such as foil and paper, can be easily deformed, so don't put pressure on them.
◦ All beads can be dusted with a soft cloth.
◦ Keep pieces in jewellery boxes or soft pouches.

COILED WIRE EARRINGS
● Coiled wire beads are highly textural, so keep your design simple to show off the beauty of the beads.
● Slightly pull out one of the coils to create a little loop for attaching a chain and an earring hook.

Tassels

✓ Tassels and trims are usually used to add finishing touches to curtains, cushions or lampshades and come in a wide variety of colours, shapes, sizes and finishes.
✓ Tassels can also be used as decorative objects on keyrings or purses.
✓ Tassels look beautiful on their own but they can be further embellished with beads.
✓ Tassels might be considered old-fashioned by some, but vintage never really goes out of fashion.
✗ Cheaper tassels may be unevenly shaped.
◉ Suede, cord, leather and chain.

Aluminium foil

✓ Aluminium foil can be formed into different bead shapes – the easiest way is to simply roll a little ball of foil.
✓ These little beads can be used just as they are, or decorated.
✓ One way to decorate foil ball beads is to attach little fluffy fabric daisies or pom-poms (or both) onto the beads using a glue gun.
✗ As foil is soft material, these beads can be easily deformed if strong pressure is applied.
◉ Medium and light beading wire, cord, ribbon, chain and elastic.

STRETCH SEQUINED BRACELET
● Sequins threaded onto elastic create a different effect and unusual texture, as only the edges of the sequins will show. You can create a little detail out of sequins in the middle of the bracelet.
● Sequins can be easily mixed with other types of beads.

Broken jewellery

✓ The majority of broken jewellery can be reused; you can turn it into funky new designs with a little imagination.
✓ Broken pieces can be linked together and they can also be used as charms on bracelets, keyrings or bag tassels.
✓ Broken pieces of jewellery can also be used for decorating different objects such as picture frames, storage boxes and gift boxes.
✗ Pieces of jewellery that are too broken or damaged are not usable.
◉ Medium and light beading wire, ribbon, cord, leather, chain and elastic.

ONE-BUTTON CHOKER
● Buttons come in different colours, sizes and shapes and are made out of different materials such as wood, shell, metal, plastic, fabric, leather and glass.
● Buttons also come in different finishes such as plain, matt or glossy; they may be carved or decorated with beads or other materials.
● Have a look in your sewing box and see if you can find and use one beautifully decorated button as a focal point on a classic choker made of ribbon.

Other materials

This chapter introduces you to the components needed to assemble your jewellery: findings such as clasps, joiners, fasteners, spacers and crimps and stringing materials such as chain, wire, string, elastic, cords and ribbon. Findings come in many different colours, shapes and sizes and they are widely available on the market for reasonable prices. Choosing the right findings and stringing materials is important so that the finish to your designs is neat and secure and in keeping with the rest of the design.

Findings and stringing materials

So far you've learned about beads, but there are other materials you'll need for beading, such as chain and wire, string and elastic and cords and ribbon. The other essential components needed to assemble your jewellery are called 'findings'.

Choosing the right stringing material

Stringing materials such as beading wire and thread, cord, ribbon, elastic, hemp, leather and suede come in many different colours, lengths and thicknesses – each is suitable for different types of designs. Much of the choice comes down to common sense, such as not threading heavy beads onto soft stringing material that will break and, conversely, not threading very light beads onto thick, heavy threading material because they won't sit well.

Usually you would choose your stringing material according to the type of beads you're using. Once you've tried out many different stringing materials, you will probably develop your own personal preferences.

Choosing your stringing material

MATERIAL AND TECHNIQUE	PROS	CONS
Flexible beading wire and crimps	° Quick and easy ° Can take heavy beads or ones with rougher holes ° Can be hidden or shown ° Ideal for beads with large or small holes	° Neat crimps can be hard to master – you may want to hide them using extra materials ° Requires special tools
Thread and knots	° Knotting has a variety of benefits both decorative and practical ° Thread is cheap and requires no expensive or bulky tools	° Can be trickier to do and takes a lot longer ° Less resistant to wear and tear ° Not suitable for very heavy beads or those with sharp holes
Cords, ribbons and yarns	° Can add a decorative look to your piece ° Can be hidden or shown ° Quick results	° Not suitable for beads with small holes ° Not suitable for beads with sharp edges ° More easily broken
Elastic	° Stringing material can be hidden ° Size of wearer not important ° Suitable for children or anyone who can't use a clasp	° Can be difficult to get a neat result
Memory wire	° Size of wearer not important ° Quick results ° Can be hidden or shown ° Suitable for children or anyone who can't use a clasp	° Some people don't like tight necklaces ° Finished jewellery has no movement or drape to it ° Ending with loops is a hard technique to master

Choosing the right findings

Jewellery-making findings are widely available, but making your own can add something special to your jewellery designs and is also cheaper. Below is a list of the most commonly used jewellery findings; these are explored in detail on the pages that follow.

° Crimps are tiny metal hollow beads used to finish your jewellery or individual beads.

° Crimp covers are metal beads that are used to cover crimps to give a finished look.

° Calottes are used to cover knots or crimps.

° Jump rings and split rings are used for connecting and linking parts of your jewellery. Jump rings are single-wire loops and split rings are double-wire loops (like a keyring).

° Wire guardians keep stringing material from wearing away, similar to French wire.

° French wire, also known as bullion or gimp, is a fine coil of wire that looks like a spring and is used for protecting thread from metal findings.

° Clasps are used to secure or connect two ends of a piece of jewellery.

° Headpins are wires with one pin end stopping the bead. They are used mainly in earrings.

° Eyepins are wires with one eye pin (small loop); they are used when you need to connect things at both ends, such as parts of dangling earrings.

° Cord ends are coils used to finish leather or suede ends. The last coil is squeezed to hold the cord tightly in place.

° Ribbon ends hold ribbon securely with small teeth, and disguise fraying ends.

° Foldover ends have two tabs folded on top of each other, suitable for finishing cord and ribbon ends.

° Cone ends are cones used for hiding the ends of different types of stringing materials, mainly on multistrand jewellery.

° Spacer bars and spacer ends are used for holding and dividing single or multistrand jewellery.

° Bead caps are used to 'dress up' beads.

° Pendant bails are used to connect a pendant to the stringing material.

° Ear wires are formed pieces of wire that fit into ear holes and hold beads.

TIP: STRINGING
Keep your stringing materials and findings in plastic bags or boxes to avoid any discolouration or damage.

Joiners, fasteners and clasps

Clasps and fasteners are used to secure or connect two ends of a piece of jewellery. Many different types of clasps are available and they are reasonably priced. They come in all kinds of colours, sizes and shapes, with or without special features and finishes. Joiners (or connectors) connect together different parts of single- or multistrand jewellery. Both clasps and joiners are easy to attach to your jewellery and easy to work with.

Types of joiners and connectors

Eyepins, jump rings, split rings and multistrand connectors are all used to attach one part of a design to another. Tube connectors and filigree connectors are threaded onto your stringing material and bridge one part of the design to another.

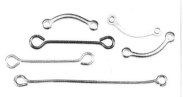

Double-loop eyepin

A double-loop eyepin is a connector with one loop on each end. They are available to buy but it is also quick and easy to make a double-loop eyepin connector.

Jump ring

Jump rings are single-wire loops that are frequently used for connecting findings to jewellery. Closed (soldered) single-wire jump rings are also available. Jump rings can also be used for chain making.

Split rings

Split rings are double-wire loops that look like mini versions of keyrings. Split rings are very stable and don't open easily, so use a split ring instead of a jump ring if you are in doubt when connecting or linking elements of a piece.

TIP: FINDINGS
To save money, reuse clasps and connectors from old and broken pieces of jewellery.

Multistrand connector

Multistrand connectors are used to connect multistrand pieces of jewellery to clasps or other sections of a piece.

Tube connector

Tube connectors are used to connect different parts of a piece of jewellery. They may be straight or curved and they can add a special and unusual look to jewellery designs.

Filigree connector

Filigree connectors are vintage-looking connectors made of soldered wire. They can impart an antique look to a piece.

Types of clasps and fasteners

When designing, it's important to choose appropriate types of clasps, joiners and fasteners to match the design and overall appearance of a piece. You also need to make sure that your fastener will support the weight of your design.

Bolt rings

Bolt rings (also known as spring rings) are the most commonly used clasps, with open or soldered tops. Large bolt rings are very easy to use, but the smaller-sized bolt rings may be tricky to operate, especially for older people.

Lobster clasp

A lobster clasp is a self-closing clasp; it can be easily opened by pushing the spring.

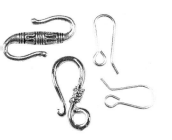

S-hook clasp

S-hook clasps are the most popular clasps as they are easy to make, they hook very well and they are simple to use.

Fish-hook clasp

In a fish-hook clasp, hoops hook around the catch and then it is pushed inside the clasp for secure fastening. These clasps work well with a range of designs. They are readily available to buy.

Toggle clasp

Toggle clasps (ring-and-bar clasps) are easy to fasten with one hand, so they are ideal for bracelets or heavy designs. The bar must pass easily through the ring, so it's important to use small beads at the ends of a project. The closed toggle clasp will shorten the jewellery, so keep that in mind when designing.

Multistrand clasp

Multistrand clasps let you attach more than one strand of the beads. They can be quite bold and striking.

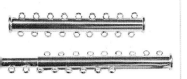

Slide-lock clasp

A slide-lock clasp has two sliding tubes that lock together, and is suitable for multistrand bracelets.

Magnetic clasp

Magnetic clasps are suitable for people with limited use of their hands. However, people fitted with pacemakers should not wear them.

Barrel screw clasp

A barrel screw clasp is a fastener consisting of two parts that screw together. This type of clasp is very easy to use.

Decorative clasp

Decorative clasps can play a major role in a design. They may be one of the main features or may simply blend in with your beads – for example, a crystal necklace might be fastened with a crystal-decorated clasp.

Spacers and metal components

Spacers and metal components are important when designing or finishing your jewellery. Spacers can lengthen or spread out your jewellery designs. They can be used as decorative accent beads or to enhance the focal beads in a piece. They can dramatically alter your design and give a more professional and unique look to your jewellery.

TIP: METAL COMPONENTS

All spacers and metal components are also available in sterling silver and gold. Obviously these options will be more expensive, but they are preferable for people with allergies.

SPACERS

These components can be very cost-effective – by using them you are effectively reducing the number of beads used in a design. They come in all different shapes, sizes, thicknesses and finishes.

Spacer beads

Spacer beads are metal beads in many sizes and shapes such as round, oval, cube, triangle, flower, animal and many more. They come in different finishes including gold, silver, antique, frosted, embossed or decorated with other materials such as beads, crystals and stones.

Spacer tubes

Spacer tubes are good for spacing out the beads on your jewellery. They come in different lengths and can be straight, curved or twisted.

Spacer bars

Spacer bars are used to space out beads and keep them in alignment in multistrand jewellery. The number of holes will match the number of strands.

Spacer rings

Spacer rings are usually large-holed beads, and are suitable for elastic bracelet designs or when working with thick stringing materials such as leather. They may also come in fancy shapes such as stars, flowers and ropes.

Bead caps

Bead caps can be used to 'dress up' your beads, but they can also extend the length of a project and change the look of a design. They may be used on one or both sides of a bead.

METAL COMPONENTS

Other metal components such as crimps, crimp covers, wire guardians, headpins and eyepins, are essential in helping you complete your designs.

Crimp beads

Crimp beads are small metal circles (or tubes) that are used to finish jewellery. They come in different sizes, but the most common ones are small (approximately 1 x 1 mm), medium (2 x 2 mm) and large (3 x 3 mm). The sizing varies according to the manufacturer.

Crimp covers

Crimp covers are used to cover crimp beads/tubes to give a neater, and more professional look.

Calottes

Calottes (also known as knot cups) are used to hide knots or crimps before attaching a clasp. They come with or without loops, and break easily if they are opened and closed too many times. They are most suitable for lightweight jewellery designs.

Wire guardians

Wire guardians are also called wire protectors, and their role is to prevent the stringing material from wearing away by reducing abrasion from the clasps. They also give jewellery a nice neat look. They look like little U-shaped channels and are quite firm, unlike French wire. They come in different sizes.

French wire

French wire, also known as bullion or gimp, is extremely fine wire made into small coils that look a bit like springs. French wire is used to protect threads from metal findings such as clasps. It is flexible, unlike wire guardians.

Headpins

Headpins are straight wires with one pin end (bar) for stopping the bead. They are used especially in making drop earrings or for attaching charms. They come in different lengths; the most common is 5 cm (2 in) long. They may come with decorated ends, for example Swarovski headpins are available.

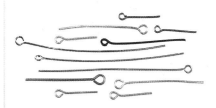

Eyepins

Eyepins are straight wires with one eyepin (small loop) and can be used as connectors (when you need to connect things from both sides of the jewellery) or for dangling earrings. As with headpins, they come in different lengths, but the 5 cm (2 in) length is mostly used.

Pendant bails

Pendant bails (pendant holders) are used to connect pendants (with holes drilled through the top of the bead) to stringing materials. There are many different types of bails such as snap-on (clipping) bails and pinch-prong bails (easy to squeeze).

Doughnut holder

Doughnut holders are bails that can easily attach/wrap doughnut beads and convert them into pendants. They come in different types such as spiral holders with smooth or textured finishes, hinged loop holders, with or without snap closure (fancy or plain) and many more.

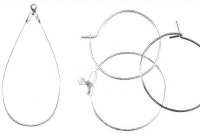

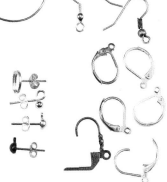

Ear wires

Ear wires are curved pieces of wire that pass through pierced earlobes. Ear wires come in different shapes:

- Hoops (circle of wire)
- Posts (straight piece of wire)
- Fish hooks (French ear wires)
- Level backs (with closure)

Ear nuts

Ear nuts are used to keep ear wires from falling off. They may be made from metal, rubber or plastic.

Clip- or screw-on earrings

Clip- or screw-on earrings are findings for nonpierced earrings where the metal is tightened against the ear with a spring or screw.

Cones

Cones are used for hiding the ends of different types of stringing materials, usually on multistrand jewellery. They come in many different sizes and shapes; the most common are cones, tubes or pressed cones. They come in different finishes, such as plain or decorated.

Cord ends

Cord ends are coils used to finish leather or suede cord ends. The last coil is squeezed to hold the cord tightly in place. The size of the coil cord end should match the size of the cord.

Crimp ribbon ends

Crimp ribbon ends are findings that hold ribbon securely with small teeth and hide fraying ends. They come in different sizes, and the size of the ribbon should match the size of the crimp ribbon end.

Foldover ends

Foldover ends have two tabs to be folded over on top of each other. They are suitable for all different types of cords, ribbons and leather. The size of the foldover ends should match the size of the threading material.

Sieves

A sieve is a metal mesh base ready for beading. Some sieves come with prong backs. Different types of sieves are available for rings, brooches, pendants, earrings and clasps. Decorated sieves make beautiful vintage-looking jewellery.

Eyeglass holder

Eyeglass holders are adjustable stretchy holders. One end can be added to beaded wire and the other to a pair of spectacles.

Chain and wire

Chain is a wonderful component for making jewellery such as necklaces, bracelets and earrings. There are many kinds of chains available in all price ranges. Wire is a vital component of many jewellery pieces and can be used decoratively or as a hidden stringing material. It is widely available in many colours, thicknesses and finishes.

DIFFERENT TYPES OF CHAINS

Chains come in different colours and finishes and are usually sold by length. The thickness and size given refer to the thickness and size of the links, for example, you might buy a 50-cm (20-in) long chain with links of 6 mm (⅜ in) long by 4 mm (⅛ in). Chains work well on their own or may be embellished with beads, charms or pendants.

Figaro chain
Figaro chain is made of a mixture of short and long flat links – usually in a pattern of one longer and two shorter ones.

Cable chain
Cable chain is a classic link chain made up of uniform round and oval links.

Box chain
Box chain is made out of links shaped like boxes or cubes connected to each other.

Bead chain
Bead chain (also known as ball chain) is made out of ball-shaped links that can either be placed close to each other or with gaps between each ball.

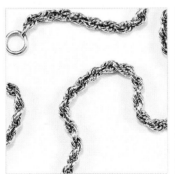

Rope chain
Rope chain is made out of oval links that are joined in such as way as to create a spiral rope effect.

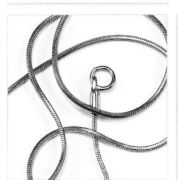

Snake chain
Snake chain (also known as Brazilian chain) is not made of links but of joined round wavy metal pieces that form a flexible tube with the appearance of a snake.

Byzantine flat chain
Byzantine flat chain is made out of flattened pairs of oval and round links formed into ancient patterns, also known as king's pattern.

Rolo chain

Rolo chain is similar to cable chain and is made out of symmetrical (round or oval) links joined together.

Curb chain

Curb chain is made out of flattened loop links joined together.

Double-loop link chain

Double-loop link chain is made out of double loops joined together.

Antique bronze chain

Antique bronze chain is made out of bronze links formed into a pattern and flattened.

WIRE

Wire is a vital component of many types of jewellery, including ear wires, headpins, eyepins, clasps and pendants. It is also used when wrapping beads, and in many other applications. Jewellery wire comes in a range of colours, sizes and thicknesses. Thickness is usually expressed in terms of mm in the UK or gauge in the US (see chart on page 137). The most commonly used wires are 0.6 mm (22-gauge) and 0.8 mm (20-gauge); however, this will depend on the nature of your project. Wires are available in different colours, but most are silver, gold, copper or brass. Wire also comes in different hardnesses; this refers to how malleable the wire is. For example, if you are making coils you would choose a soft wire that is easy to manipulate. But if you are making earring hooks that need to keep their shape, you might go for half-hard or hard wire. Most of the beading projects in this book use silver-plated wire, which is easy to use and relatively cheap. Precious wires are much more expensive, so only start to use them when you are more experienced.

TIP: CHAIN

You can easily make chain using different types of jump rings linked in various interesting patterns.

Types of wire

A number of different types of wire are used in jewellery making, from the commonly used silver-plated wire to wire with special qualities like memory wire.

Silver-plated wire

Silver-plated wire is the most common jewellery wire – it's widely available and reasonably cheap. It is suitable for making jewellery findings such as headpins, eyepins and clasps, and for wire wrapping. Silver-plated wire is usually made out of copper and plated with sterling silver. Some people are allergic to silver-plated wire, though antiallergenic nickel-free versions are now available.

Gold-plated wire

Gold-plated wire is also a commonly used jewellery wire, usually made out of copper and plated with gold. Gold-plated wire is used in the same way as silver-plated wire, and gold-plated nickel-free wire is also available.

Memory wire

Memory wire is made from heat-treated steel; it is a very strong and hard wire so it is important to use strong wire cutters to trim it. Memory wire is preformed wire that keeps its shape and is suitable for making bracelets that fit any size and don't need a clasp.

Knitted wire

Knitted wire (also called knitted ribbon) is a preknitted wire that comes in different colours and sizes. It is easy to stretch, twist and form. Beads can be threaded onto knitted wire or wrapped inside it. Many knitted wires are free of nickel (check with the manufacturer).

Brass and copper wire

Brass and copper wire are good for practising and maquettes because they are soft and inexpensive.

Fancy wire

Fancy wires are colour-coated wires based on copper. They are easy to shape and are suitable for making jewellery and wire beads, or may be used for other types of crafts.

Precious metal wires

Sterling silver is 92.5% silver and 7.5% copper, and is stamped with the number 925. Sterling silver is relatively expensive and it can tarnish over time. Pure gold wire is very expensive and quite hard to find.

Wire thicknesses

Jewellery wire is available in a variety of thicknesses. It's a good idea to use the right thickness of wire for the job because it will give better results and be easier to work with.

0.3 mm (28-gauge) wire

0.3 mm (28-gauge) wire is very fine, suitable for wire crocheting, wire knitting or for decorating sieves.

0.4 mm (26-gauge) wire

0.4 mm (26-gauge) wire is easy to bend and twist, and is therefore suitable for wire crocheting or wire knitting projects. This wire is often used for making twisted-wire tiaras.

0.5 mm (24-gauge) wire

0.5 mm (24-gauge) wire is not as easy to bend as 0.4 mm (26-gauge) wire but is also not as hard as 0.6 mm (22-gauge) wire, therefore it is suitable for making headpins or eyepins for beads with small holes.

0.6 mm (22-gauge) and 0.8 mm (20-gauge) wires

0.6 mm (22-gauge) and 0.8 mm (20-gauge) are the most commonly used wires, suitable for making jewellery findings such as clasps, ear wires, headpins and eyepins, for bead wrapping, and many more applications.

1 mm (18-gauge) and 1.25 mm (16-gauge) wires

1 mm (18-gauge) and 1.25 mm (16-gauge) are sturdy and firm wires suitable for making clasps for heavy jewellery, large jump rings or coiled charms.

1.5 mm (14-gauge) and 2 mm (12-gauge) wires

1.5 mm (14-gauge) and 2 mm (12-gauge) are very thick wires, suitable for making firm shapes such as bangles or rings.

Wire profiles

Wire comes in several shapes. A selection of these are shown below (left–right): oval, diamond, square, round and rectangular.

Bead-stringing wire

Bead-stringing wire is a nylon-coated, flexible and durable, but strong beading material. (Beading wire is not jewellery wire, as mentioned in the chain and wire section, see page 79.) Bead-stringing wire consists of several twisted strands of stainless steel, and the flexibility of the wire depends on the number of strands – more strands mean more flexibility.

see page 79

TIP: WIRE
Wires work very well with crimps and other metal components.

Bead-stringing wire comes in different colours, but the most popular ones are gold or silver. A well-known and very strong beading wire is tigertail. This is best to use with heavy beads with rough holes, but it can also be used for all kinds of other projects, though it is not recommended for use with pearls. Tigertail is much cheaper than other beading wires, but it does kink easily. Some well-known beading wire brands include Beadalon, Soft Flex and Accu-Flex. Your choice of brand and thickness will depend on your project and personal preference. Sterling silver and gold beading wires are also available, but they are much more expensive.

Strands

Lots of people get confused when it comes to choosing the right type of wire. Here is some advice about how to read the information displayed on the reel label.

49-strand jewellery wire

49-strand jewellery wire (made up of 49 strands) is the softest and most flexible kind of wire, equally good for small, light beads (such as pearls) and for larger semiprecious stones. This wire doesn't kink and is suitable for professional-looking jewellery designs, especially bracelets, because it is extremely flexible. This wire is the most expensive type, except for precious beading wires such as sterling silver and gold.

19-strand jewellery wire

19-strand jewellery wire (made up of 19 strands) is a soft wire with good flexibility, suitable for working with seed beads, pearls, glass beads and semiprecious stones. It is great for jewellery projects such as necklaces, bracelets and earrings – easy to work with and kink and abrasion resistant. This wire is slightly cheaper than 49-strand wire but more expensive than 7-strand wire.

7-strand jewellery wire

7-strand jewellery wire (made up of seven strands) is a strong, soft and flexible wire that is fairly kink resistant (more so than tigertail). This wire is suitable for general jewellery designs, but is especially good for heavy beads, beads with sharp-edged holes or designs that do not require a high level of flexibility. This type of wire is cheaper than 49- or 19-strand wire.

Diameter

The diameter of the wire can affect its resistance – the larger the diameter, the less resistance. In other words, thicker wire has less resistance than thinner wire. The most commonly used wire diameter is 0.4 mm (26-gauge). Beading wire should fill as much of the bead hole as possible. For example, small-diameter 0.25 mm (30-gauge) wire will be suitable for seed beads and large-diameter 1 mm (18-gauge) wire will be suitable for beads with large holes.

Wire (actual diameter)	Diameter	Size	Suitable Bead
————	0.30 mm (0.012 in)	XS	Seed beads – small beads
————	0.38 mm (0.015 in)	S	General beads – general holes
————	0.46 mm (0.018 in)	M	General beads – general holes
————	0.91 mm (0.036 in)	L	Beads with large holes

Length

Beading wires come in different lengths, which may be specified in feet, metres or both. The length of the wire will be written on the spool label. Beading wires usually come in lengths of 5 m (16.4 ft), 9.2 m (30 ft), 30.5 m (100 ft) or 305 m (1,000 ft) – this depends on the manufacturer.

Other stringing materials

Stringing materials other than beading wire include string, fibre, cord, ribbon and elastic. When choosing a stringing material, your considerations will include the type of project you are planning (you might be after a specific look), the future wearer (they might be allergic to metal) and the size of the holes in the beads you'll be using.

Nylon and silk threads

Nylon threads are a modern alternative to traditional silk threads. They are mainly used in bead-weaving designs and for traditional beadwork. Silk thread is typically used for stringing pearls; knots are tied between each bead. Nylon and silk threads are strong, but not as stretchy and flexible as other stringing materials. They may break if the maximum tension is exceeded, especially during knotting. Nylon and silk are available in many attractive colours and in different thicknesses. Some threads come with stainless steel needles.

TIP: STRINGING

• Keep silk and nylon threads in plastic bags or containers to avoid any discolouration.
• Do not use these threads for heavy bead designs.

Illusion cord

Illusion cord is clear, and is mainly used for making 'floating' necklaces using pearls (see page 50), or with glass or crystal beads. Illusion cord can be knotted and comes in different thicknesses.

TIP: STRINGING

Some fishing lines can be used for making floating necklaces, but be aware that fishing line doesn't have the same durability as illusion cord. Use clear-dry jewellery glue on top of your knots to keep them from coming undone.

Elastic cord

Elastic cord is ideal for making stretchy jewellery that can be easily slipped on and off, such as bracelets, hair-bands or children's jewellery. Elastic cord is also a great option for making jewellery for people who are allergic to metal and cannot wear clasps or any other metal findings. Elastic cords come in different colours and thicknesses.

TIP: STRINGING

When tying knots in elastic, tie them under slight tension to keep them from coming undone. Use clear-dry glue on top of your knot. To hide knots, use beads with large enough holes to slide over them at the end.

Habotai Foulard cord

Habotai Foulard cord originally comes from China. It is silky, smooth and comfortable to wear. This type of cord comes in many different colours and sizes, and is often referred as 'second skin' cord due to its soft, silky feel.

TIP: STRINGING

Habotai Foulard cord can be a little slippery to work with, but it looks stunning with a single pendant threaded on it.

Leather and suede cords

Leather and suede cords are among the oldest threading materials; they are natural and flexible. Leather cords are typically round while suede cords are flat. They come in many different colours and thicknesses. Leather and suede cords are suitable for modern or traditional jewellery.

TIP: STRINGING

• Leather and suede cords are not suitable for beads with small holes.
• They can be finished with an adjustable sliding knot.

Ribbons

Ribbons are often associated with special moments when gifts are exchanged, such as birthdays, Christmas and weddings. Ribbons come in many different colours, patterns and textures. They can be combined with different types of beads and findings. Using ribbons can completely change the final look of your design.

TIP: STRINGING

To keep ribbon from fraying, try cutting the ends diagonally or heating them with a flame to melt and seal the edges. (This can be done with a candle or a lighter.)

Techniques and essential projects

Now it's time to put everything you've learned into practice. In this chapter, each project introduces a new technique, varying from a simple strung bracelet to a more complex beaded wire pendant. One or two variations accompany each piece, and show how changing colours, proportions, size or type of bead can alter the design.

The beader's toolkit

Choosing the right tools will directly impact the quality of the jewellery you make. Working with the right tools will also increase your enjoyment of making jewellery and save you time.

Different beading techniques will require different types of tools. For example, for bead weaving all you need is a beading mat, scissors, needles and glue. The quality of the tools is important, but you do not have to spend a fortune when starting. It is important to use tools only with the materials for which they are designed – for example, do not use side cutters to cut memory wire as you can easily damage the cutting edges – instead, use appropriate memory-wire cutters or shears. Some household items can stand in for tools, such as bulldog clips instead of bead stoppers, or a wooden spoon instead of a forming mandrel.

Pliers

Pliers are used for shaping, bending, straightening, crimping, gripping and countless other purposes. They are an essential part of a jewellery designer and maker's kit.

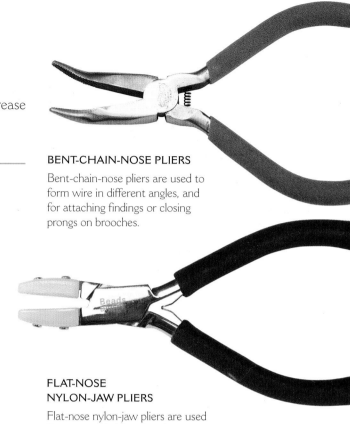

BENT-CHAIN-NOSE PLIERS

Bent-chain-nose pliers are used to form wire in different angles, and for attaching findings or closing prongs on brooches.

FLAT-NOSE NYLON-JAW PLIERS

Flat-nose nylon-jaw pliers are used for gripping, holding, bending or straightening wire while keeping the surface of the wire from being scratched.

CHAIN-NOSE PLIERS

Chain-nose pliers are used for gripping, holding and bending wire, and crimping crimps, such as the tiny crimps on 'floating' necklaces.

ROUND-NOSE PLIERS

Round-nose pliers are used for shaping wire and creating loops and curves, for example when making eyepins, clasps or loops on earring hooks.

FLAT-NOSE PLIERS

Flat-nose pliers are used for gripping, holding, bending or straightening wire, such as for straightening headpins.

HALF ROUND PLIERS

These pliers can be used for forming earring hooks or to bend rings into shape.

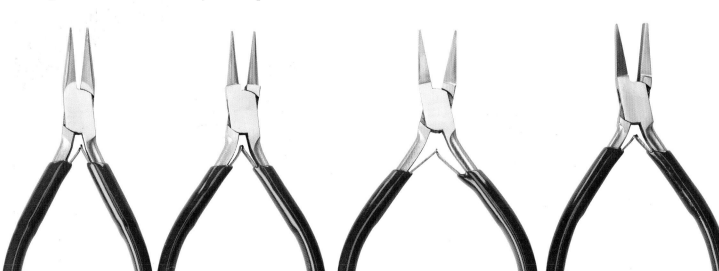

CRIMPING PLIERS

Crimping pliers are used for attaching and forming crimps and can be also used for a neat finish when wrapping loops.

Wire cutters

There are two main types of wire cutters: side and end. These should be sufficient for most wire work; however, for thick, hardened wire, such as memory wire, special memory-wire cutters can make things easier.

SIDE CUTTERS

Side cutters are used for precision cutting or when you need to cut off tiny pieces from wire-wrapped ends on earrings or pendants.

THREE-STEP WIRE-LOOPING PLIERS

Three-step wire-looping pliers have a top jaw with three different-sized steps for creating identical loops over and over again, such as when making jump rings.

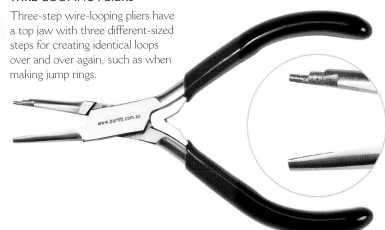

www.burfitt.com.au

END CUTTERS

End cutters are used for cutting thicker wire and are much stronger than side cutters.

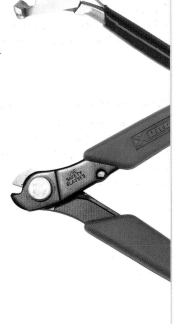

MEMORY-WIRE CUTTERS

Memory-wire cutters (shears) are used for cutting thick hardened tempered wire (up to 2 mm/12-gauge), such as memory wire.

Serrated pliers

Never use pliers that have serrated jaws. These will grip into your wire, marking it and ruining the surface. If these are all you have to hand, you can wrap masking tape around the jaws as a temporary measure.

Other tools and equipment

In addition to pliers and wire cutters there is a wealth of equipment available to the bead and wire jewellery designer. From mandrels, used for forming jump rings and wire loops to bulldog clips, which can be used to temporarily secure an unfinished project.

REAMER

A reamer is used to make bead holes bigger or smoother. It comes with three different-sized diamond tips stored inside the hollow handle. Use it carefully to avoid breaking your beads. It can be used underwater if necessary, especially with glass or natural beads.

Flat head for smoothing rough surfaces

Slim tip for clearing a hole

Conical tip for widening the ends of drill holes

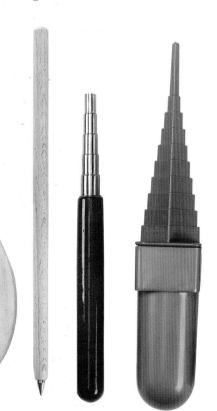

MANDRELS

Mandrels are used for forming different shapes in wire, such as jump rings, charms or joiners. Different types of mandrels are available, including round, square or triangular. You can also shape wire using makeshift tools, for example a wooden spoon or a round pencil can be used for forming the loops on earring hooks.

DIAMOND NEEDLE FILES

Diamond needle files are used to file the ends of pieces of wire, for example the ends of ear wires, so that they do not scratch the wearer.

TWEEZERS WITH SHOVEL

These tweezers are used for picking up beads; the shovel helps you to scoop up small seed beads in one go. They can also be used for clearing beads from the bead mat after you have finished work.

SCISSORS

Sharp scissors are used for cutting thread quickly and neatly in tight spaces.

THREAD CUTTER

A thread cutter can be worn around your neck like a pendant for ease of use while you are working.

STEEL CROCHET HOOKS

Steel crochet hooks are used for wire crocheting and they come in different sizes. Crocheting with wire is hard on your fingers and can be quite a challenging project, but will make for beautiful and unique jewellery.

NEEDLES

Needles are mainly used for beadwork projects using small seed beads. There are many different types of needles:

• Big-eyed needle – easy to thread as the eye runs through most of the length of the needle.

• English needle – very thin, flexible and the most commonly used needle. This needle is perfect for working with seed beads with tiny holes.

AWL

An awl or large needle is ideal for moving knots to where you want them.

BEAD STOPPERS AND BULLDOG CLIPS

Bead stoppers and bulldog clips are used to keep beads from falling off the ends of the stringing material, prior to crimping or finishing.

THREAD ZAP AND LIGHTER

A Thread Zap or a lighter is used for burning away unwanted thread ends or sealing the ends of ribbons to keep them from fraying.

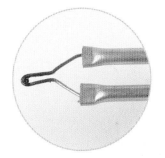

HAMMER AND MINI-ANVIL

A hammer and mini-anvil are used for adding texture or flattening wire; the anvil is a steel block with a flat surface for hammering and also has two horns (flat and round) for bending or forming wire around.

GLUE AND CLEAR NAIL POLISH

Glue and clear nail polish stick items together and can be used to seal knots.

JIG

A jig is used for making decorative wire shapes. Its pegs can be arranged to whichever positions you need and it is particularly useful if you want to make the same shape time and again.

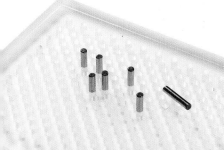

Chunky turquoise memory bracelet

Threaded with silver, glass and semiprecious beads

Memory wire is a stainless steel wire, which will always spring back into shape when expanded or released. Usually it is sold in six- or 12-loop packs, but you may find packs with larger numbers of loops. Different diameters, usually 'large' or 'small', are available. It's important to use memory wire shears or hard wire cutters to cut memory wire, as it can easily damage general wire cutters. In this project, bracelet memory wire is used and treated as a threading material, rather than a general wire. As memory wire can expand easily, and does not need a clasp, it will fit any size of wrist. So this technique is perfect if you are not sure about the size of the wearer's wrist, or are making these items to sell to others.

MATERIALS AND TOOLS

- *30 of 13 x 18 mm chalk turquoise beads – pear-shaped, side-drilled*
- *90 of 3 mm (size 6) silver seed beads*
- *60 of 4 x 8 mm antique silver carved bicone spacer beads*
- *92 of 2.5 mm gunmetal beads*
- *30 of 4 mm silver plain bead caps*
- *6 loops of small memory wire*
- *Round-nose pliers*
- *Memory wire shears or hard wire cutters*

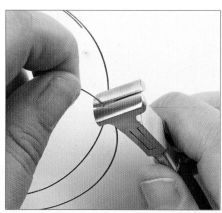

1 If your memory wire has not been precut into coils, use memory wire shears or hard wire cutters to cut your wire so that it is one long continuous strand of six loops. When cutting, you will find it easier if you cut the wire on the left or right side of the cutter, rather than putting the wire in the middle of the cutting blade.

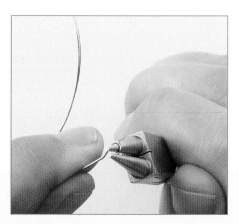

2 Use round-nose pliers to create a closed loop at one end of the wire. To create a closed loop, put the end of the wire between the jaws of a pair of round-nose pliers. Twist the pliers around until the wire becomes a complete 'closed' circle.

Semiprecious beads	**40%**			
Silver	**60%**			
	a	b	c	d

a Size 6 seed beads
b Plain bead caps
c Bicone spacers
d Gunmetal beads

Variation: Round beads ▷

The pear-shaped turquoise beads have been replaced with round beads. Using round beads will soften the bracelet and will also weigh less. Silver spacer beads are placed in a different order to make a different pattern.

Semiprecious beads	**30%**			
Silver	**70%**			
	a	b	c	d

a Size 10 seed beads
b Size 6 seed beads
c Bicone spacers
d Spacer rings

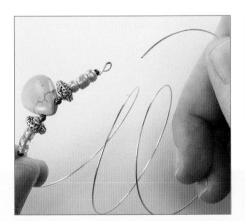

Use a closed loop to secure the end of the bracelet.

3 When threading the beads onto the memory wire, push the beads to the very end of the wire, up to the closed loop that you just created in Step 2. The closed loop will keep the beads from falling off. The semiprecious and glass beads are quite heavy, so they may stretch the wire a little; this is the reason for using a smaller memory wire size.

4 Thread the beads onto your wire, following the repeating pattern pictured top left, until all six wire loops are fully beaded. Stop threading when you have around 1 cm (⅜ in) of wire left at the end, and create another closed loop as you did in Step 2.

See also
Semiprecious beads, page 48
Chain and wire, page 79

Elastic bead bracelet

Acrylic elastic bracelet; easy to make and wear

Elastic is a versatile material – often used for children's jewellery, men's bead bracelets and for people who cannot wear metal clasps. Elastic is available in many different sizes and colours. It can stretch easily, so for heavy beads, it is advisable to use more than one loop of elastic, and choose beads with larger holes to accommodate them. These loops are known as 'rounds'.

MATERIALS AND TOOLS

- *10 of 22 mm acrylic ball beads*
- *1 m (1 yd) of 0.5 mm clear elastic*
- *Glue*
- *Big-eye needle*
- *Small bulldog clip*

1 Cut 1 m (1 yd) of clear elastic and secure one side with the bulldog clip to keep the beads from falling off the elastic while you are working. Thread all of your beads onto the elastic.

2 Once you are done, carefully remove the bulldog clip. Push your beads up the elastic so you have around 15 cm (6 in) of empty elastic at the end where the bulldog clip was. Tie this elastic to the elastic directly above the other end of your beads.

Variation: Coin beads

Use the same technique, but
a totally different bead.
These coin-shaped beads,
with added silver spacers,
give a very different look.

| Acrylic beads | **90%** | | |
| Silver | **10%** | Spacer beads | |

See also
Plastic and acrylic beads, page 58
Other stringing materials, page 83

3 You need to tie two tight knots, leaving about
10 cm (4 in) of your 15 cm (6 in) empty, still. You
will of course have lots of elastic left on the other
side. You are now going to use this elastic to make
the bracelet stronger.

4 Thread the shorter piece of elastic through one or
two beads and put a bulldog clip onto the end. Now
take the longer piece of elastic and thread it through all
of the remaining beads, going in the opposite direction
to the shorter piece of elastic. When the two ends of
elastic meet, tie knots again as you did in Step 2, and
then repeat Step 3. If you are having difficulties
threading the elastic, use a big-eye needle.

5 Once you have done your third set of knots, dab
some glue onto the third knot to give it a little
more strength. Make sure no glue gets on the beads.
Once it's dry, cut off any remaining elastic.

Simple strung bead necklace

Combining silver with pale glass beads

Stringing is the one of the first beading techniques you will learn. The best way to start is with a single-strand bead necklace – as these are quick and easy to make. Stringing beads means passing stringing material through the holes of beads.

To avoid a disappointment, always buy a few more beads than you think you will need.

MATERIALS AND TOOLS

- 5 of 15 mm and 4 of 10 mm green glass beads
- 2 of 15 mm silver decorated metal beads
- 4 of 7 mm silver decorated metal spacer beads
- 10 of 4 mm silver decorated metal spacer beads
- 14 of 2 mm round silver metal spacer beads
- 12 of 20 mm metal curved tube beads
- 2 crimp beads
- 2 calottes
- 1 toggle clasp
- Beading wire
- Glue
- Bead stopper or bulldog clip
- Flat- and round- nose pliers
- Crimping pliers
- Wire cutters

Glass beads	50%		
Silver	50%		
	a	b	c

a Tube beads
b Large spacer beads
c Small spacers, clasps, etc.

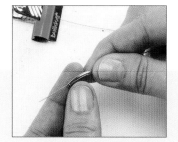

1 Secure your beading wire with a bulldog clip or bead stopper (there is nothing worse than your beads running away!). Plan your pattern first and then thread all of your beads onto the wire. By leaving both ends open (but secured with the bulldog clip), you can still remove, add to or adjust your design at this stage.

2 Keep the bulldog clip on one of the ends of your necklace and free the other one. Slide on one calotte followed by a crimp and close the crimp at the very end of the wire with your crimping pliers. Make sure that the wire goes through the whole length of the crimp and, if necessary, cut off any excess wire.

3 Move the calotte to the end of the wire and pull gently to test it – the calotte should stop firmly once it hits the crimp. The crimp must be sized to go inside the calotte without it coming out of the end. Once your calotte is placed firmly around your crimp, hold it there and apply a little glue.

4 Wait for the glue to set and then close the calotte using crimping pliers. Hold it in this position for a few seconds to make sure that the calotte is holding together nicely.

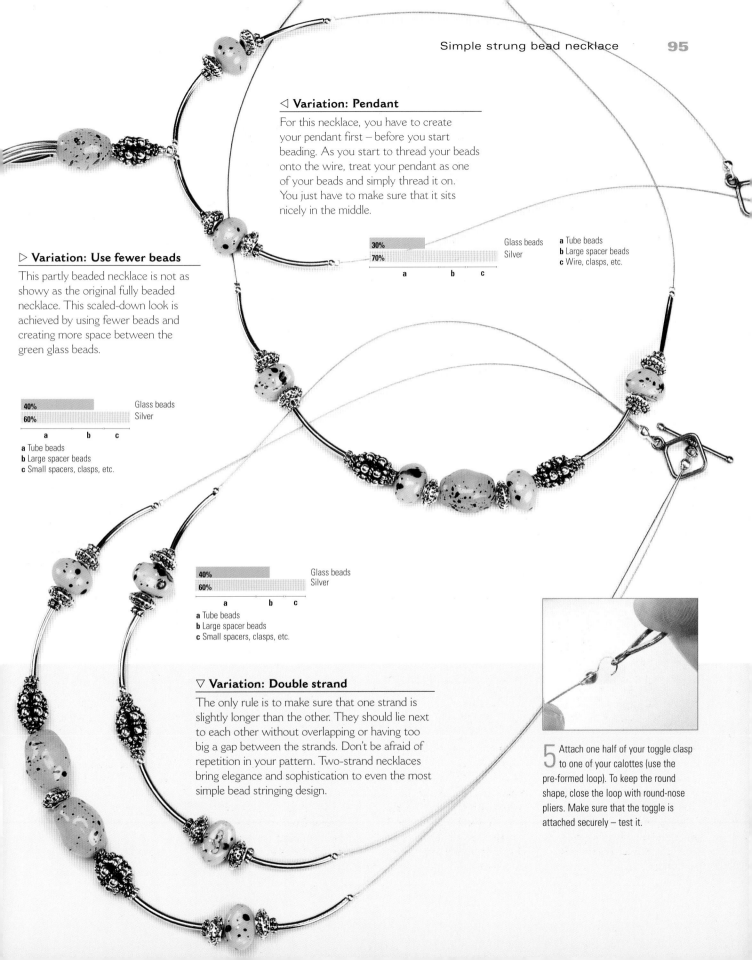

◁ Variation: Pendant

For this necklace, you have to create your pendant first – before you start beading. As you start to thread your beads onto the wire, treat your pendant as one of your beads and simply thread it on. You just have to make sure that it sits nicely in the middle.

30%			Glass beads	**a** Tube beads
70%			Silver	**b** Large spacer beads
a	**b**	**c**		**c** Wire, clasps, etc.

▷ Variation: Use fewer beads

This partly beaded necklace is not as showy as the original fully beaded necklace. This scaled-down look is achieved by using fewer beads and creating more space between the green glass beads.

40%			Glass beads
60%			Silver
a	**b**	**c**	

a Tube beads
b Large spacer beads
c Small spacers, clasps, etc.

40%			Glass beads
60%			Silver
a	**b**	**c**	

a Tube beads
b Large spacer beads
c Small spacers, clasps, etc.

▽ Variation: Double strand

The only rule is to make sure that one strand is slightly longer than the other. They should lie next to each other without overlapping or having too big a gap between the strands. Don't be afraid of repetition in your pattern. Two-strand necklaces bring elegance and sophistication to even the most simple bead stringing design.

5 Attach one half of your toggle clasp to one of your calottes (use the pre-formed loop). To keep the round shape, close the loop with round-nose pliers. Make sure that the toggle is attached securely – test it.

Single-drop earrings

Make a pair of earrings from scratch – including the hooks

Women can never have enough earrings; every outfit deserves a matching pair. When you are designing your earrings, consider a few elements such as colour, length, weight, metal allergies, hairstyle, occasion and so on. These earrings are a great starting project, and later on you will find that the techniques shown here can be used for other projects such as pendants and charms as well. It's important to use the correct pliers to get a professional finish.

MATERIALS AND TOOLS

- 4 of 3 mm silver flower spacer beads
- 2 of 8 mm green clear glass rondelle beads
- 2 of 10 mm clear doughnut beads
- 2 of 10 mm green clear coin beads
- 2 of 3 mm light green clear ball beads
- 2 of 50 mm (2 in) silver headpins
- 0.8 mm (20-gauge) silver wire
- Wire cutters
- Needle file
- Round-nose pliers
- Chain-nose pliers
- Ball-peen hammer and anvil
- Wooden spoon

Bead note

- This bead has a clear front and back, but is lined with silver around the edges. To ensure that the bead will work for your design, check which way the hole is drilled.

Glass beads	10%	10%	70%
Silver	10%		
	a	b	

a Flower spacer beads
b Wire hook

Glass beads	40%		10%
Silver	50%		
	a	b	c

a Wire hook
b Bead lining
c Flower spacers

◁ **Variation: Beaded hooks**

You can make your plain earring hooks more interesting by adding small beads to them. Remember to add your beads before hammering the back of the curve.

1 Using wire cutters, cut two 6 cm (2 in) pieces of 0.8 mm (20-gauge) silver wire. File one end of each piece of wire flat. (You only need to file one end because the other end will be cut later on when you adjust the length of the earring hooks you are about to make.)

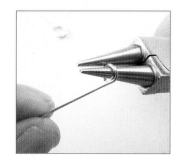

2 First you need to create a closed loop, which will be at one end of the earring hook. Place the filed end of wire between the two jaws of your round-nose pliers, 0.5 cm (3/16 in) down from the nose of the pliers. To create your closed loop, twist the pliers around until the wire becomes a complete 'closed' circle. Repeat for the second earring.

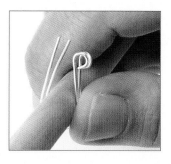

3 Hold both wires next to each other with the loops facing towards you. Place them in front of a wooden spoon (you could also use a large rounded pencil or other rounded object). Hold the wire firmly with your main hand and form a loop by wrapping the wire around the wooden spoon, until both ends are pointing upwards.

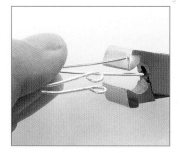

4 To adjust the length of both earring hooks, place both hooks on top of each other to see if one hook is longer than the other. Cut off any excess wire at the straight ends, if needed, so that they are both the same length. To avoid injury, cover the wire with your free hand when cutting so if any wire flies up into the air when you cut it, it will not hit you in the face. File both straight ends until they are smooth.

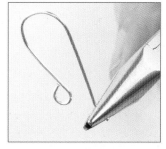

5 Form a little 'tail' at the end of the earring hooks using chain-nose pliers. Make sure that angle of the tail is not too big so it won't be difficult to push the earring hooks through the ear holes.

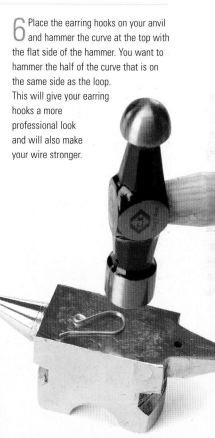

6 Place the earring hooks on your anvil and hammer the curve at the top with the flat side of the hammer. You want to hammer the half of the curve that is on the same side as the loop. This will give your earring hooks a more professional look and will also make your wire stronger.

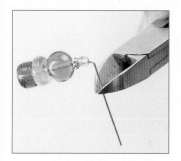

7 Thread your beads onto the headpins and bend the wire to a 90-degree angle from the top bead. Trim the wire, leaving about 1 cm (3/8 in) of wire free.

8 Grasp the end of the wire with your round-nose pliers and turn the wire into a loop without losing your 90-degree bend. Make sure that the loop is closed on the top of the bead. You can always adjust the loop if necessary.

9 You are now going to attach the beads to your earring hooks. Hook your beads onto the earring by putting the earring hook loop through the closed loop on the bead headpins. If there is not enough space to be able to do this, use your round-nose pliers to open a small gap on your earring hook loop. Once the beads are attached, close the loop on your earring hook securely, again using your round-nose pliers, so that the beads cannot escape.

> **See also**
> Glass beads, page 44
> Chain and wire, page 79

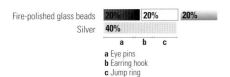

Fire-polished glass beads
Silver

20%	20%	20%
40%		

a   b   c

a Eye pins
b Earring hook
c Jump ring

Dangling earrings

Earrings made by linking eyepins and jump rings

Designing dangling earrings can take time, but it's fun and you can create unique, eye-catching pieces with personality, much like the person who is going to wear them. Big earrings don't necessarily have to be heavy, and keep in mind that heavy earrings can stretch your earlobes and cause irritation – choose your beads wisely.

MATERIALS AND TOOLS

- *12 of 10 mm black, white, and clear fire-polished Czech glass beads*
- *12 of 4 mm silver plain caps*
- *6 of 50 mm silver eyepins*
- *2 of silver jump rings*
- *Earring hooks (see page 97)*
- *Wire cutters*
- *Round-nose pliers*
- *Chain-nose pliers*
- *Needle file*
- *Ball-peen hammer and anvil*

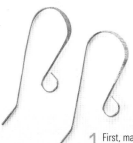

1 First, make your own earring hooks. If you haven't done this before, instructions on how to do this can be found on page 98 (Single-drop earrings).

2 Now lay out your design before you make anything, so that you get a clear understanding of how these earrings will fit together. First, put your earring hook down in front of you. Then below this, put one eyepin, with the eye facing down, and then put two more eyepins below this, sticking out at opposite angles with the eyes at the top. The shape should look like the one shown here. Once you are happy with the design, thread your beads onto the eyepins.

3 Take the eyepin that will join with your hook. Create a closed loop at the straight end. For instructions on how to create closed loops see page 97 (Single-drop earrings).

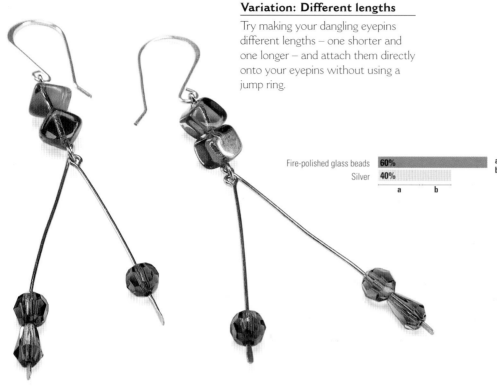

Variation: Different lengths

Try making your dangling eyepins different lengths – one shorter and one longer – and attach them directly onto your eyepins without using a jump ring.

See also

Glass beads, page 44
Spacers and metal components, page 76

Fire-polished glass beads	**60%**		**a** Eyepins
Silver	**40%**		**b** Wire hook
		a b	

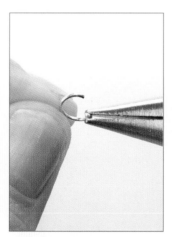

4 Now take your other two eyepins, which you have threaded the beads onto. Hammer the straight ends of the wire, so they become flat. Hammer the wire until it becomes wide enough to keep your beads from falling off. You may need to test it and hammer a few times.

5 Hold your jump ring with flat chain-nose pliers close to the cut of the ring. Open it slightly to create a small gap, by pulling one side of the jump ring up towards you, rather than pulling the sides apart. You can use two sets of pliers to do this if necessary.

6 Place your top beaded eyepin and two dangling parts onto the jump ring and close the jump ring securely by bringing the two ends together with no gap between them.

7 Place round-nose pliers inside the small loop on your earring hook and open it slightly, just enough to slip your beaded eyepins onto it. When this is done, close the loop securely. Now, repeat Steps 1 to 7 for the other earring.

MATERIALS AND TOOLS

- 50g of pink/red glass bead selection
- 21 of 6 mm silver bicone spacers
- 22 of 5 mm silver flower spacers
- 22 of 4 mm silver flower spacers
- Beading wire
- 1 twister silver clasp
- 2 small silver crimps
- Chain-nose pliers
- Small bulldog clip
- Wire cutters

Fully beaded necklace

From long to short, with a twist

Long fully beaded necklaces are fun to make and can be completed in a short time. By using a mixture of beads, you can have a random pattern, making them quick to thread. They can be worn in two ways: long, or short – by twisting them and adding a twister clasp.

1 Cut the desired length of beading wire, secure one end with a bulldog clip and start threading your beads in a random pattern.

2 When the wire is fully beaded, string two small crimps on one end of the wire and pass the other end of the wire through both crimps.

3 Pull both sides of the wire until both crimps are next to each other and there is no space between the beads on either end. Squeeze both crimps firmly with chain-nose pliers.

Glass beads	10%	10%	10%	10%	10%	10%	10%	5%
Silver	25%							

Small   Large
Spacer beads

Variation: Using up leftovers

Have you ended up with lots of leftover beads in different shapes and colours? Why not use them to make a beautiful, colourful, long necklace? Use silver spacers now and then, to unite these disparate beads together. These kinds of necklaces go very well with long maxidresses or with plain outfits that need a bit of colour.

Glass beads	40%	40%	5%
Silver	15%		

a b c

a Bicone spacers
b Flower spacers
c Twister clasps

See also
Glass beads, page 44
Bead-stringing wire, page 82

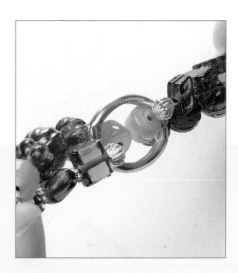

4 Cut off any spare wire. Your long fully beaded necklace is now ready to wear, but it can also be worn as a short necklace – go to Step 5.

5 Stretch your long necklace out and then twist both ends together in opposite directions.

6 Clip both ends of the necklace together using the silver twist clasp.

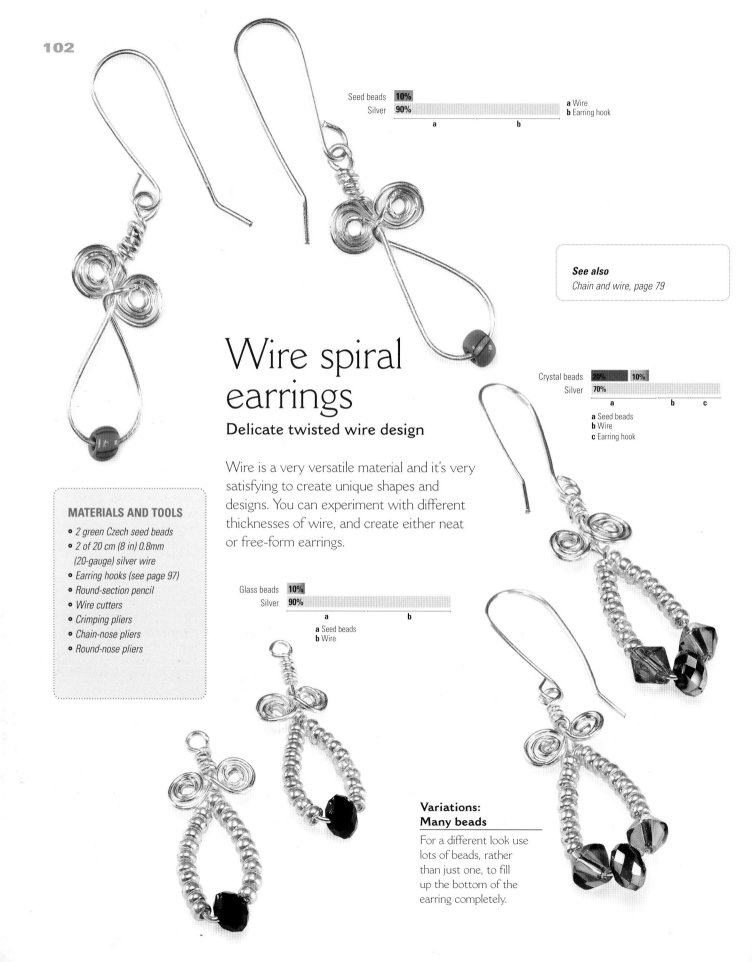

Seed beads	10%			**a** Wire
Silver	90%			**b** Earring hook
		a	**b**	

See also
Chain and wire, page 79

Crystal beads	20%	10%			
Silver	70%				
		a		**b**	**c**

a Seed beads
b Wire
c Earring hook

Wire spiral earrings

Delicate twisted wire design

Wire is a very versatile material and it's very satisfying to create unique shapes and designs. You can experiment with different thicknesses of wire, and create either neat or free-form earrings.

MATERIALS AND TOOLS

- *2 green Czech seed beads*
- *2 of 20 cm (8 in) 0.8mm (20-gauge) silver wire*
- *Earring hooks (see page 97)*
- *Round-section pencil*
- *Wire cutters*
- *Crimping pliers*
- *Chain-nose pliers*
- *Round-nose pliers*

Glass beads	10%		
Silver	90%		
		a	**b**

a Seed beads
b Wire

Variations: Many beads

For a different look use lots of beads, rather than just one, to fill up the bottom of the earring completely.

1 Cut one 20 cm (8 in) piece of silver wire; place a small green bead in the middle of the wire. Fold the wire (keeping the bead in the middle) over a round-section pencil or similar object. Cross the two ends of the wire above the pencil and form a wrap.

2 Grasp one of the wires with round-nose pliers and turn the tips of the pliers to make a small circle just above the wrap. Try to make it as round as possible.

3 Hold the circle tightly with flat-nose pliers and start to form a spiral by curling the wire around the circle. Stop forming your spiral when you have gone around the circle three times and make sure that the remaining wire is facing upwards.

4 Repeat Steps 2 and 3 for the remaining length of wire so that you end up with two spirals next to each other.

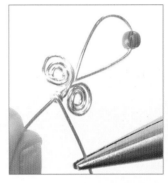

5 Twist one wire around the other wire two or three times, to form tiny circles that wrap around one wire. These should be small and close to each other. It doesn't matter which wire you use to do this.

6 Cut any leftover wire off the wire that you twisted. Squeeze the cut end with chain-nose pliers to get rid of the sharp edge.

7 Grasp the remaining wire with your round-nose pliers about 5 mm (³⁄₁₆ in) away from the circles you just created, and make a loop. Wrap the remaining wire under this loop, to make more circles that go down towards the circles you just created.

8 Once you are done, trim off the end of the wires if necessary, getting as close to the stem as you can, using wire cutters.

9 Use crimping pliers (or chain-nose pliers) to smooth the wire back, to ensure there are no sharp ends.

10 Attach the earrings to your earring hooks. You can use store-bought hooks or you can make your own by following the instructions on page 97 (Single-drop earrings).

Crystal cube earrings

'Beaded beads' – making a big bead from little beads

The main ingredients for this project – creating three-dimensional cubes – are beads, needles, and thread. For different effects, experiment with different sizes and colours of beads. You will need 12 beads to create each cube.

MATERIALS AND TOOLS

- 24 of 5 mm bicone glass beads
- Dark red nylon thread
- 2 silver wire guardians
- Earring hooks
- Clear nail polish
- 2 size 10 beading needles
- Scissors
- Round-nose pliers

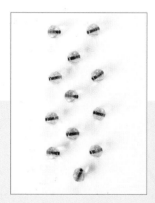

1 Lay out 12 glass beads in the pattern pictured.

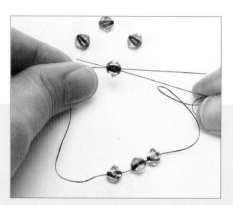

2 Cut 60 cm (24 in) of thread and thread each end on a needle. Thread on the first three beads and place them in the middle of the thread. Pick up the fourth bead and, using your needles, put the thread through the bead from both sides. As you pull the thread tight the beads will form a small square.

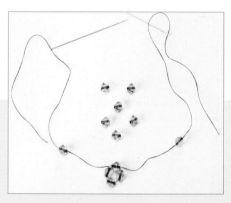

3 Thread your fifth bead on one needle and the sixth bead on the other needle. Push the beads up to your other four beads.

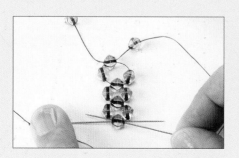

7 Now all 12 beads are beaded, you are going to join them together. Go back to your first bead and, using your needles, put the thread through the bead from one side and then put it through from the other side.

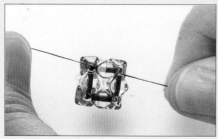

8 Pull the thread firmly to form a cube. Pass your thread several times through other beads to secure your cube and give a tight finish.

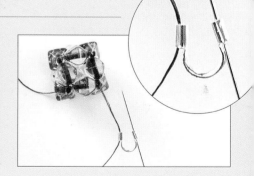

9 To attach your cubes to the earring hooks you need a loop. In this case your wire guardian is going to be the loop. Thread both needles through the closest two beads and pass each needle through the wire guardian and back through the beads.

△ Variation: Embellished cubes

Decorate your cubes by threading additional beads around the outside of the cube.

Glass beads **45%**
Silver **55%**

a   b   c

a Earring hook
b Seed beads
c Wire guardian

See also
Glass beads, page 44
Other stringing materials, page 83

Glass beads **50%**
Silver **50%**

a   b

a Earring hook
b Wire guardian

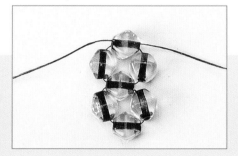

4 Pick up the seventh bead and, using your needles, put the thread through the bead from one side and then put it through from the other side. Then pull the thread tight; again, the beads will form a small square.

5 Thread the eighth bead on one needle and the ninth bead on the other needle. Push the beads up against the other beads.

6 Pick up the tenth bead and, using your needles, put the thread through the bead from one side and then put it through from the other side. Then pull the thread tight. Finally, thread the eleventh bead on one needle and the twelfth bead on the other needle. Push the beads up against the other beads.

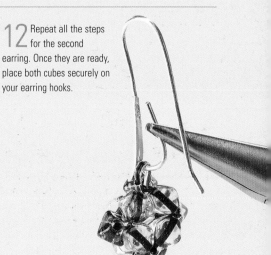

10 Repeat this process a few times to securely attach the wire guardian. If your two threads are not next to each other, thread one of them back through the beads until they are. Tie two knots.

11 Place nail polish on the knot and let it dry. Once dry, cut off any remaining thread.

12 Repeat all the steps for the second earring. Once they are ready, place both cubes securely on your earring hooks.

Chain charm bracelet

Combining bead clusters and chain links

This project involves a few techniques, but the main objective is to learn how to connect these different elements together: forming links, attaching charms, making your own clasp and joining it to the chain.

Semiprecious beads	50%		
Silver	50%		
	a	b	c

a Chain
b Bead caps
c Clasp

Variation: Gold chain

If you prefer a gold finish, simply replace the silver chain, silver spacer beads and silver bead caps with gold ones.

Semiprecious beads	50%		
Gold	50%		
	a	b	c

a Chain
b Bead caps
c Clasp

MATERIALS AND TOOLS

- 8 of 5 mm silver spacer flower beads
- 7 of 10 mm red round jasper beads
- 8 of 8 mm red round jasper beads
- 19 of 4 mm red round jasper beads
- 14 of 8 mm decorated silver bead caps
- 28 of 4 mm plain silver bead caps
- 1 mm (18-gauge) silver wire
- Approx. 25 cm (10 in) of 13 x 7.5 mm silver chain
- Silver headpins and eyepins
- Chain-nose pliers
- Round-nose pliers
- Flat-nose pliers
- Wire cutters
- Needle file
- Hammer and anvil
- Ruler

1 First, create your bead links. Take one eyepin and thread on the beads in the following order:
- plain bead cap
- 4 mm red round jasper bead
- decorated silver bead cap
- 10 mm red round jasper bead
- 8 mm decorated silver bead cap
- 4 mm red round jasper bead
- plain bead cap

Bend your eyepin 90 degrees above the plain bead cap leaving about 1 cm (⅜ in) length of wire. Use wire cutters to cut the remaining wire.

2 Using the round-nose pliers, roll the wire up to form a loop. It takes two movements to do this. First, roll the wire around the tip of the pliers with one turn, making sure that you are not lifting up the bend you've just created. Next, go back to the end of the loop – making sure you are inside it – and make another turn, this time aiming to close the loop above the beads.

3 Make another two sets of bead links in the same way, so that you end up with three of them in total.

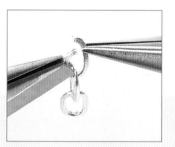

4 The chain is quite hard to open, so you'll need two pairs of pliers – chain-nose pliers and flat-nose pliers. Chain links are like jump rings, used in other projects found in this book, but they are usually tougher and in a preformed link/chain. Grasp the third link of your chain with both pliers and open it slightly in the same way that you would open a jump ring – by pulling one side of the jump ring up towards you, rather than pulling the sides apart.

5 Using the technique from Step 4, prepare the other sets of linked chain:
- 1 x two links
- 2 x three links
- 1 x five links

6 Connect your bead links to your chain links, starting with five chain links on one side and two links on the other side of the bracelet and three links between each of the bead links. Follow the instructions in Step 4 for opening and closing the links when joining them together.

7 To create a small end charm, place a plain bead cap, a 4 mm red round jasper bead, and a plain bead cap on a headpin and make a little loop above the bead.

8 Place this end charm at the end of your five chain links. The end charm will give a professional finish to the end of the bracelet.

9 Make three charms by using the technique from Step 1, but instead of three eyepins, use three headpins. For two of the charms thread your beads onto your headpins in this order:
- plain bead cap
- 8 mm red round jasper bead
- 5 mm silver spacer flower bead
- 4 mm red round jasper bead
- plain bead cap

Do this for two of the headpins. For the third (middle) headpin charm, thread your beads on in this order:
- 8 mm decorated silver bead cap
- 10 mm red round jasper bead
- 8 mm decorated silver bead cap
- 4 mm red round jasper bead
- plain bead cap

Prepare another three sets of these, so that there are four in total.

10 Attach your first headpin charm set onto a chain link just in front of your first bead set.

11 Now attach your next headpin charm set onto a chain link between the first and second bead set. Repeat this pattern further down the chain, until all of your headpin sets are attached.

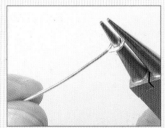

12 Now you need to make your clasp. Cut a 4 cm (1½ in) length from your 1 mm (18-gauge) silver wire and file one end of the wire smooth. Place the filed end inside your round-nose pliers and form a closed loop. At first, this will look a little like an eyepin.

13 Approximately 5 mm (³⁄₁₆ in) below the loop, grasp the wire with the round-nose pliers. Using your fingers, push the wire away from you, 180 degrees around the pliers.

14 With flat-nose pliers, make a little tail at the end of the wire, pointing away from the loop. If you have too much wire at the end, trim it using your wire cutters. It's important to file the end of the tail smooth; otherwise the clasp may cut the wearer or catch on clothes.

15 Attach the clasp to the shorter end of the bracelet. The longer chain on the other side will give you flexibility to adjust the length of the bracelet, by hooking the clasp to any of the chain links.

See also
Semiprecious beads, page 48
Chain and wire, page 79

Three-strand bracelet
Crimping ends and attaching toggles

This project uses a toggle clasp, so that the bracelet is easy to put on. Antique gold will give the finished bracelet a particularly elegant look.

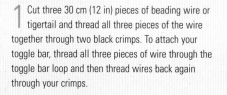

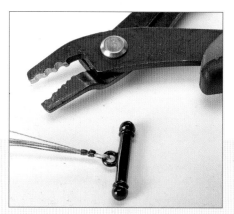

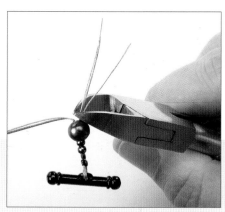

1 Cut three 30 cm (12 in) pieces of beading wire or tigertail and thread all three pieces of the wire together through two black crimps. To attach your toggle bar, thread all three pieces of wire through the toggle bar loop and then thread wires back again through your crimps.

2 Push the crimps down the wire, so that they are close to the toggle bar and form a neat loop. Use the crimping pliers to crimp the crimps. To do this, first use the second (zigzag) hole from the top of the crimping pliers, and then use the first (round) hole – squeezing the crimps each time. Test your crimps to ensure they are securely attached.

3 Thread all the beading wires through two 2 mm black metal spacer beads and one 5 mm antique gold round spacer bead. Cut off the remaining wire, if necessary, from the shorter lengths of wires sticking out from the crimps.

Toggle	5%		
Glass beads	35%	40%	
Antique gold	20%	**a** Spacer beads	

a

Variation: Silver finish

Replace the antique gold
with silver for a more
casual look.

Glass beads	40%	40%	
Silver	20%		

a   **b**

a Spacer beads
b Toggle clasp

See also

Joiners, fasteners and clasps, page 74
Spacers and metal components, page 76

4 Thread your beads onto each of the individual
beading wires, as shown.

5 Join the beading wires together again and thread
them all through a 5 mm antique gold round spacer
bead, two 2 mm black metal spacer beads, two black
crimps, and a toggle loop. Then thread the beading
wires back again through your crimps, metal spacer
beads and antique gold spacer bead. Pull the beading
wires to leave a small, neat loop above the toggle loop.

6 Cut off any remaining beading
wire as neatly as you can.

Crochet beaded bracelet

Delicate loops of fine wire, beaded

If you've never crocheted before, you may like to try this with cotton thread first and then with a soft wire, before you move onto stronger wire. This is optional, but it will allow you to become more familiar with the techniques involved. Wire will not stretch and will not wrap itself around the hook like cotton will. To crochet with beads – thread your beads onto the wire first and push them towards the reel. The softer wire (approximately 0.3 mm [28-gauge]) could be used for small, light beads and the stronger wire (0.4 mm [26-gauge]) for large, heavy beads.

See also
Chain and wire, page 79

Semiprecious beads	60%		
Silver	40%		
	a	b	c

a Wire
b End bars
c Clasp and jump rings

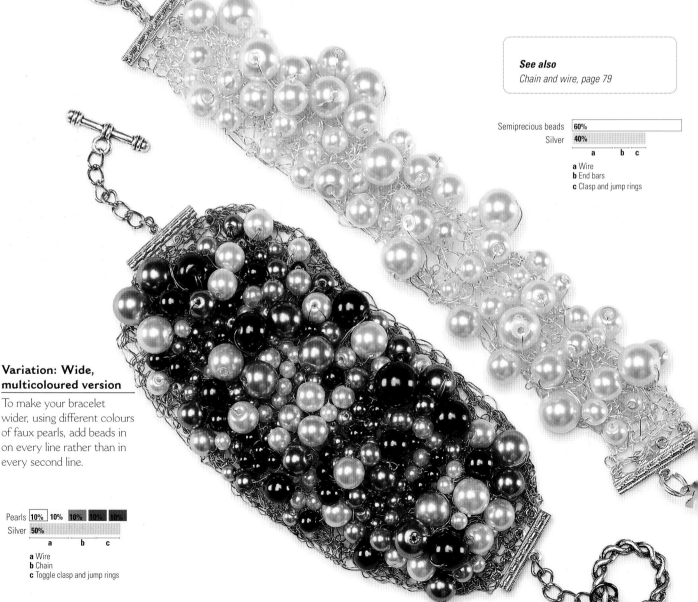

Variation: Wide, multicoloured version

To make your bracelet wider, using different colours of faux pearls, add beads in on every line rather than in every second line.

Pearls	10%	10%	10%	10%	10%
Silver	50%				
	a		b	c	

a Wire
b Chain
c Toggle clasp and jump rings

1 Thread all the beads onto the wire in size order, smallest first, and push them towards the reel.

2 Thread the wire twice through the four rows on the end bar, leaving a short end. Wrap this short end securely around your base wire.

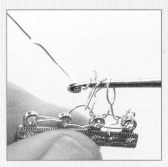

3 Hold the bar in one hand and form a loop close to the first row of the end bar.

4 Wrap the loose wire around the crochet hook and draw back through the wire between the first and second rows, forming a second loop. You will end up with two loops.

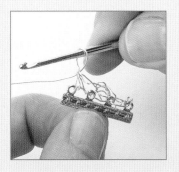

5 Wrap the loose wire around the crochet hook and draw it back through both loops. Now you will be left with just one loop.

6 Repeat Step 3 and continue until you've come to the end and formed your links. Create two or three rows of joined links, making sure that the wire is neither too tight nor too loose.

7 Bring your first bead close to the links and continue forming other links. The bead should be captured inside your new link now.

8 Move another bead close to the link and continue until you come to the end of the row. Then form one line of links without beads. Now repeat – adding beads in every second line. Make sure the beads are all on the same side.

9 When you've bead-crocheted the full length of the bracelet (approximately 13 cm/5 in – depending of the size of the wearer's wrist), form two or three rows of non-beaded links (see Step 6) and attach the other four rows of the end bar by firmly passing the wire through the bar's rows, joining your links. Once securely attached, cut off any remaining wire, leaving a short end, which needs to be securely wrapped around the base.

10 Open the split ring slightly and attach it to the end bar, along with your clasp, as shown.

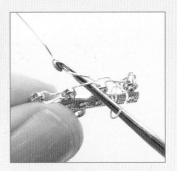

11 On the end bar, on the other side of the bracelet, attach another split ring and the other end of the clasp.

Long chain necklace
Clear the head without need for a clasp

This project uses beaded links and split rings, along with a variety of lengths of chain, to create a more personal and less uniform style of necklace. Depending upon the beads you choose, you can create a variety of styles to suit any outfit. This is a relatively easy project, using the chain and split rings to link the sections together, and simple loops to create the beaded links. It can be worn doubled around the neck, or wrapped around the wrist to create a funky, modern bracelet.

MATERIALS AND TOOLS

- 10 of 8 mm semiprecious (lapis) round beads
- 20 of haematite spacers in five different shapes
- 10 gunmetal eyepins
- 20 of 5 mm gunmetal split rings
- 8 of 7 mm gunmetal split rings
- 115 cm (45 in) length of 4 mm gunmetal chain
- Wire cutters
- Round-nose pliers
- Flat-nose pliers
- Chain-nose pliers
- Needle file
- Ruler
- Pencil

See also
Chain and wire, page 79

1 Take one eyepin; slide a haematite bead onto the pin, followed by a lapis bead and finally a matching haematite bead.

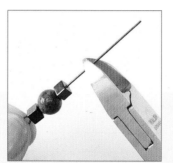

2 Take the ruler and cut the eyepin around 7 mm (⅜ in) from the end of the last haematite bead, using the cutters. File any rough pieces from the cut edge.

3 Take the round-nose pliers and mark with a pencil either side of where the eyepin loop sits on the pliers.

4 Recreate that size of eye at the other end of the pin by making a right-angled bend close to the bead. Place the tip of the wire between the round-nose pliers where you have marked, and rotate the pliers to start the loop. Reposition the pliers to allow you to continue to rotate the pliers until the tip meets the wire. Continue Steps 1 to 4 until you have created all ten beaded links.

8 Attach a 5 cm (2 in) length of chain to one of the beaded links with the 5 mm split ring as in Step 7. Attach the third beaded link.

9 Repeating the technique from Steps 7 and 8, attach another 5 cm (2 in) length of chain and than attach a 7 mm split ring.

Round lapis beads	30%		
Dark grey	70%		
	a	**b**	**c**

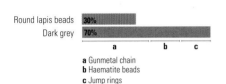

a Gunmetal chain
b Haematite beads
c Jump rings

Variation: Multicoloured beads

Use colourful glass beads to create a fun and bright contrast to the gunmetal chain. The use of multiple colours draws the eye around the necklace. Using lapis creates a glamorous eveningwear style, whereas using wooden beads would create a more natural, everyday style.

Glass beads	10%	10%	10%	10%
Dark grey	60%			
		a	**b**	**c**

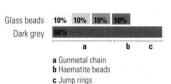

a Gunmetal chain
b Haematite beads
c Jump rings

5 Add a 5 mm split ring to both ends of the beaded links.

6 To create the different lengths of chain needed, take the chain-nose pliers and take hold of one side of the link, then with the flat-nose pliers, grip the other side of the link and push it forwards and away from you. This opens the link. Do not pull the link apart sideways; this may break the metal or it may lose its shape and not go back together correctly. Close the link once the selected length is detached from the main length of chain. Create the following lengths:

- 1 x 3 cm (1⅛ in)
- 4 x 5 cm (2 in)
- 1 x 5.5 cm (2³⁄₁₆ in)
- 4 x 6 cm (2⅜ in)
- 3 x 6.5 cm (2½ in)
- 1 x 7 cm (2¾ in)
- 1 x 7.5 cm (3 in)
- 2 x 8 cm (3⅛ in)
- 1 x 8.5 cm (3⅜ in)

7 Take the 3 cm (1⅛ in) length of chain and connect a beaded link to either end of the chain using the 5 mm split rings. You can either open the end chain link using the two pairs of flat-nose pliers, slipping the split ring on and closing the link again. Or you could slide the chain onto the split ring, by opening the split ring slightly and slipping the chain on until it is fully on the split ring.

10 Keep attaching links in this order:
- 6.5 cm (2½ in) length of chain
- beaded link
- 6.5 cm (2½ in) length of chain
- 7 mm split ring
- 6 cm (2⅜ in) length of chain
- 7 mm split ring
- 5 cm (2 in) length of chain
- beaded link
- 7.5 cm (3 in) length of chain
- 7 mm split ring

- 5.5 cm (2³⁄₁₆ in) length of chain
- beaded link
- 8 cm (3⅛ in) length of chain
- beaded link
- 6 cm (2⅜ in) length of chain
- beaded link
- 8.5 cm (3⅜ in) length of chain
- 7 mm split ring
- the final piece of chain is 7 cm (2¾ in) in length. Attach the other end of the chain to the first beaded link and you have completed your necklace.

Sieve-based ring
Combining silver with sparkling seed beads

Sieve-based rings, also known as statement rings or bling rings, are fashionable right now. Using sieves is an established technique though, also used for making brooches and pendants. Sieves are usually made from metal with predrilled holes and they come in many shapes, colours and sizes. Most sieves are available with a metal back or lid.

MATERIALS AND TOOLS

- *1 ring sieve*
- *4 button shape silver beads (all different sizes)*
- *11 disc-shape black beads*
- *10 g of size 11 gold seed beads*
- *10 g of size 8 black seed beads*
- *Needle size 12*
- *Needle threader (if needed)*
- *Nylon thread (grey) – Dandy Line or Power Pro recommended*
- *Clear nail varnish*
- *Glue*
- *Flat-nose pliers*
- *Scissors*

Bead note

- *Make sure the beads are on top of the convex sieve not sitting inside it.*

Disc beads	5%		
Glass beads	20%	10%	
Silver	65%		
		a	b

a Button beads
b Base ring

1 Thread nylon onto your needle (preferably a short length of nylon and a short needle for easy work). If necessary use a needle threader. With lightweight threads use double or even triple strands. Make a knot at the end of two strands and put a little bit of clear nail varnish on your knot to secure the thread end. Let it dry and cut off any excess thread.

2 The beads should be sitting on the top, not inside of the sieve. Start by securing your thread: make a few stitches through two holes around one central hole on the sieve until the thread is secure. Tie the thread at the back of the sieve (give it a hard pull to ensure it is secure).

3 Bring the thread up through the centre hole and thread on the button beads, from the largest to the smallest one. Next, thread on one black disc-shape bead and one gold seed bead. Go back through the disc-shaped bead and all button beads, then through the centre sieve hole. Pass the thread back through all the beads and the sieve a few more times to make secure.

4 Use the second row of holes on the sieve edge. Bring the needle out through each of these holes in turn, threading on one disc-shape bead secured with a gold seed bead on the top, then back through the disc bead and the sieve. Repeat, using the same thread, until you have all 10 sets of beads in place. If the beads feel loose, go back through the sieve again to further secure them.

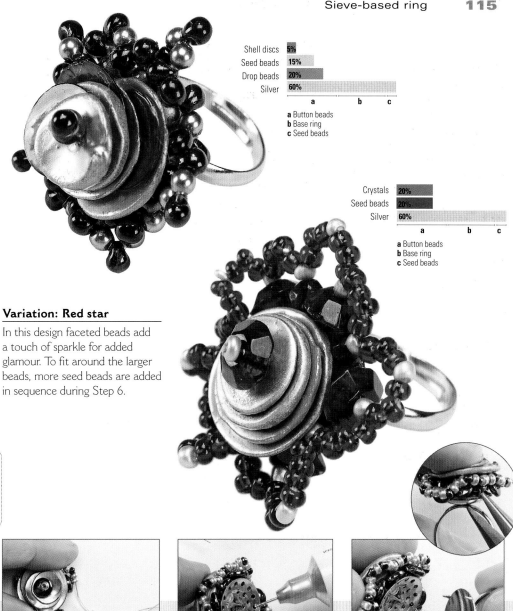

Shell discs	**5%**		
Seed beads	**15%**		
Drop beads	**20%**		
Silver	**60%**		
	a	**b**	**c**

a Button beads
b Base ring
c Seed beads

Crystals	**20%**		
Seed beads	**20%**		
Silver	**60%**		
	a	**b**	**c**

a Button beads
b Base ring
c Seed beads

Variation: Purple cluster

This ring uses exactly the same technique as described below to make the black and gold combo, but this version introduced purple drop-shaped beads and a tone of this same colour – light purple – for the lighter tones. Purple is also boosted in the shell discs, which have beads layered between the silver button beads – you can use any flat bead with a central hole to make this design.

Variation: Red star

In this design faceted beads add a touch of sparkle for added glamour. To fit around the larger beads, more seed beads are added in sequence during Step 6.

See also
Seed beads, page 66
Spacers and metal components, page 76

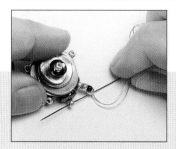

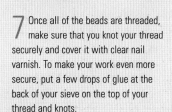

5 Make sure that the gold seed beads are facing out so you can easily get into their holes. Bring the thread out through one of the gold seed beads. Start to add three seed beads (gold, black, gold) and then pass the needle through the next gold seed bead.

6 Thread five seed beads (gold, black, gold, black, gold) and pass it though the next gold seed bead. This will create a little wave. Carry on until you thread through all of the initial 10 gold beads. Keep in mind that you need a little room for small prongs on your ring base, so make sure that you are not working too near to the edge of the sieve.

7 Once all of the beads are threaded, make sure that you knot your thread securely and cover it with clear nail varnish. To make your work even more secure, put a few drops of glue at the back of your sieve on the top of your thread and knots.

8 Attach the beaded sieve onto your ring base, with the prongs (teeth) sitting comfortably around the sieve. Use flat-nose pliers to fold each prong (tooth) into the sieve and allow your glue to set. Be careful not to scratch the surface of your ring base or break any beads.

Knitted wire necklace

Flexible fine wire bead carriers

MATERIALS AND TOOLS
- 5 of 10 mm light gold faux pearl beads
- 70 cm (28 in) of light gold knitted jewellery wire
- 2 large gold crimps
- 1 decorative gold clasp
- 6 of 6 mm gold rings
- Chain-nose pliers
- Wire cutters

Knitted wire can be easily twisted and stretched to form different shapes. It can stretch up to three times its original width or length. The structure of the wire allows you to thread beads on the outside of the wire or wrap them inside the wire. Other wires or beading materials can be added and clasps are easily attached.

Knitted wire	25%
Pearl beads	25%
Gold rings	25%
Clasp crimps	25%

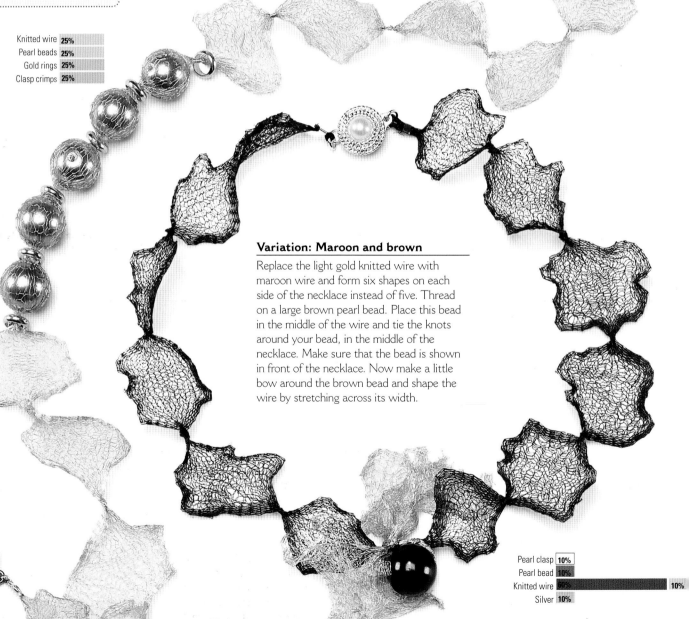

Variation: Maroon and brown

Replace the light gold knitted wire with maroon wire and form six shapes on each side of the necklace instead of five. Thread on a large brown pearl bead. Place this bead in the middle of the wire and tie the knots around your bead, in the middle of the necklace. Make sure that the bead is shown in front of the necklace. Now make a little bow around the brown bead and shape the wire by stretching across its width.

Pearl clasp	10%
Pearl bead	10%
Knitted wire	80%	10%
Silver	10%

1 Stretch and twist the end of your wire, creating a small roll.

2 Thread a large crimp and one part of your clasp onto the roll, and then thread back through your crimp.

3 Squeeze the large crimp into place with your chain-nose pliers. Make sure that the clasp is securely attached, and cut off any excess wire.

4 Stretch across the width of your wire by using both hands to form a new shape.

5 Twist the end of your new shape.

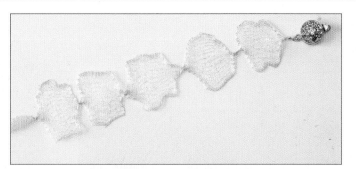

6 Continue to make another four new shapes with twists at the end – five in total.

7 Thread on a 6 mm gold ring and push it close to your last shaped form.

8 Open the end of the wire, and stuff the 10 mm gold pearl inside the wire.

9 Push the gold pearl close to the gold ring.

10 Twist the wire end of the large gold pearl bead and thread on another gold ring. Continue to do this until you've threaded on all five beads.

11 Following the instructions from Step 2 and 3, form another five new shapes on the other side of the beads. Attach the other side of the clasp by following instructions from Step 2.

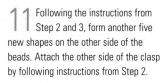

See also
Seed beads, page 66
Spacers and metal components, page 76

Fabric bead and ribbon necklace

Fabulous, different and quick to make

Large round and oval fabric beads are great for chunky jewellery, with endless possibilities for mixing and matching, and ribbon complements these beads perfectly. For a different, fabulous yet gentle look, the larger oval beads have been customized by sewing fabric flowers onto them. This project takes less than hour to make and you don't need perfect sewing or any other jewellery making techniques to achieve a great result.

MATERIALS AND TOOLS

- 2 of 7 mm red fabric beads (Chinese knot)
- 2 of 15 mm red fabric beads (Chinese knot)
- 1 of 20 mm round red/gold fabric beads
- 2 of 25 mm oval red/gold fabric beads
- 2 of 5 mm round antique gold metal beads
- 110 cm (1 yd) of 3 mm gold satin ribbon
- 6 small red fabric flowers
- Glue
- Ruler
- Scissors
- Red nylon thread
- Lighter
- Needle

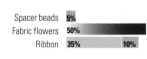

Spacer beads	5%	
Fabric flowers	50%	
Ribbon	35%	10%

1 Sew the bottoms of the three little red flowers together with red nylon thread. Keep the thread and needle attached.

2 Now all three flowers are together, place them at the end of one of the oval red/gold beads, close to the large hole. Hold them firmly and start sewing them on. Make a few knots after sewing and place a dab of glue on the top of your knot.

3 Trim one end of the ribbon with scissors into a long, sharp point. To reduce fraying, hold the end of the ribbon next to a lighter flame to seal the end. Take care not to burn the ribbon or set it alight.

Variation: Black and silver

Replace the 3 mm gold satin ribbon with 6 mm black satin ribbon, and replace the red/gold fabric beads with 30 mm black/silver round beads. Different shaped acrylic silver and gunmetal spacer beads can be added between and around the fabric beads. The sheer dark fabrics will contrast with the silver beads, giving the necklace a modern look.

Acrylic beads **25%**
Fabric beads **50%**
Ribbon **25%**

4 String the beads onto the trimmed end of the ribbon in the following order:
- antique gold metal bead
- 15 mm red fabric bead
- oval red/gold bead (flowers facing backwards)
- 7 mm red fabric bead (Chinese knot)
- 20 mm round bead
- 7 mm red fabric bead (Chinese knot)
- oval red/gold bead (flowers facing forwards)
- 7 mm red fabric bead
- antique gold metal bead.

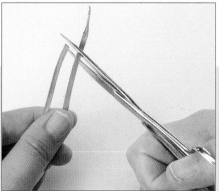

5 Place the beads in the middle of the ribbon and cut both ends of the ribbon with scissors. Again, seal the ends using a flame.

6 Once you are done, tie the necklace around your neck and tie the ends together with a bow.

See also
Fabric-covered beads, page 64
Other stringing materials, page 83

Decorative bead	10%		
Semiprecious turquoise	20%		
Suede cord	20%		
Silver	50%		
		a	b

a Wire
b Toggle clasp and cord ends

Semiprecious stone-and-wire pendant

An unusual wire pendant on a leather cord

Handcrafted semiprecious stone pendants wrapped into wire are quite magnificent and unique. In this project you'll learn how to work with two different thickness of wire, how to attach spring cord ends at the ends of leather and suede cord and how to attach a toggle clasp.

MATERIALS AND TOOLS

- 2 of 20 mm semiprecious turquoise beads
- 1 of 20 mm silver round decorative beads
- 55 cm (21¾ in) of 3 mm turquoise suede cord
- 90 cm (35½ in) of 1 mm (18-gauge) silver wire
- 90 cm (35½ in) of 0.6 mm (22-gauge) silver wire
- 2 of 4 mm spring cord ends
- 2 of 7 mm jump rings
- 1 of 20 mm silver toggle clasp
- Ruler
- Needle file
- Wire cutters
- Round-nose pliers
- Chain-nose or crimping pliers

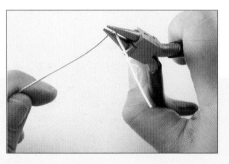

1 File the ends of the silver wire flat. Place your round-nose pliers 3 cm (1⅛ in) from the end of the wire. Bend the wire towards you, until it is bent at a 90-degree angle.

2 Wrap the wire around the top jaw of the pliers until you have created a loop.

Variation: Coral beads

Semiprecious coral beads have been used in this variation project with matching dark red leather cord and toggle clasp. The wire flower petals have been squeezed more tightly and lightly hammered on the top to give a different finish.

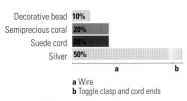

Decorative bead	**10%**
Semiprecious coral	**20%**
Suede cord	**20%**
Silver	**50%**

a   b

a Wire
b Toggle clasp and cord ends

Bead note

- *This decorative silver bead adds an extra texture and gives an antique look to your pendant.*

See also
Chain and wire, page 79
Other stringing materials, page 83

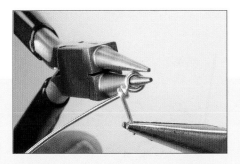

3 Hold the loop inside the pliers and wrap the wire tightly around itself about three times, beneath the loop, to form small circles. Cut off any remaining wire with the wire cutters. Use the tip of the chain-nose pliers or crimping pliers to neatly squeeze the end of the wire.

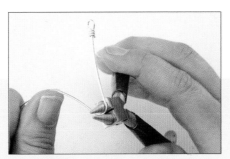

4 Position the round-nose pliers 4 cm (1½ in) below the wrap and bend the wire at a 45-degree angle.

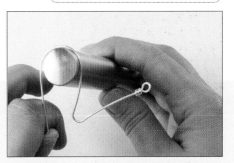

5 Use a round metal bar or other round object to create your first flower petal. Position the wire against your metal bar about 3.5 cm (1⅜ in) away from the bend. Hold the wire firmly with your thumb and push the wire around the bar to form a loop. This is the top of the petal.

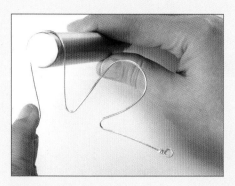

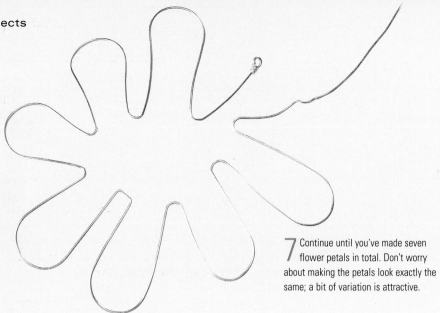

6 Place round-nose pliers about 3.5 cm (1⅜ in) away from the top of the petal and bend the wire again with the round-nose pliers. Repeat Step 5 to create the second flower petal.

7 Continue until you've made seven flower petals in total. Don't worry about making the petals look exactly the same; a bit of variation is attractive.

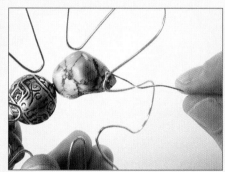

11 Thread on your beads in the following order: 20 mm semiprecious turquoise bead; 20 mm silver decorative bead; 20 mm semiprecious turquoise bead.

12 Push the beads towards the other wraps and keep them as tight as possible. Now secure the wire, just below the fourth petal.

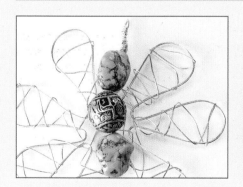

15 Continue wrapping the 0.6 mm (22-gauge) wire until you have decorated all seven petals. When you're done, wrap the end of the wire securely and cut off any remaining wire.

16 Cut 55 cm (21¾ in) of 3 mm turquoise leather cord. Bend about 0.5 cm (³⁄₁₆ in) of the end of the leather cord and push both parts into the 4 mm spring cord end. You can use the tip of the chain-nose pliers to help you to do this.

17 Use the chain-nose pliers to squeeze the last row of the spring cord end. Check that it is securely attached.

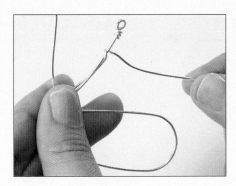

8 Place the two ends of the wire next to each other and start wrapping the loose wire around the other wire, starting from about 1.5 cm (⅝ in) below the existing wrapping. Work up toward the existing wrap, until both wraps meet.

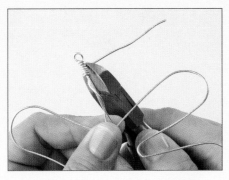

9 Cut off any remaining wire with wire cutters and use the tip of your chain-nose pliers or crimping pliers to neatly squeeze the end of the wire.

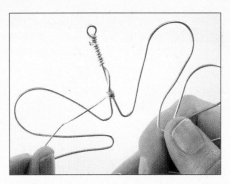

10 Attach a new 0.6 mm (22-gauge) wire, just below the newest wrap. Wrap it twice around the two 'petal' wires.

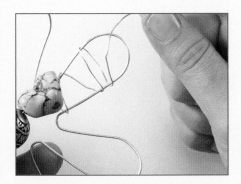

13 Now wrap this wire around the fourth petal, as shown.

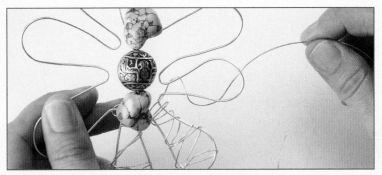

14 Work the wire back to the centre of your flower, and then repeat the pattern on the next petal. The patterns do not need to be exactly the same – mix it up a little!

18 Place the pendant on the leather cord and attach the other spring cord end to the other end of the leather cord (remember to place the pendant on the leather cord first).

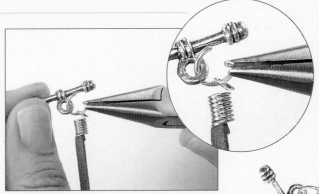

19 Use two 7 mm jump rings to attach a toggle clasp to the spring cord ends. Open the jump ring slightly (see page 99). Place the spring cord end and one part of the toggle clasp onto the jump ring and close it securely.

20 Attach the other part of the toggle clasp in the same way on the other side.

Variation: Colour

Lighter and different coloured beads have been used for this variation. Copper findings have been replaced with silver ones and two different colour silk cords (dark pink and grey) have been used instead of one.

Wire beaded pendant

Twisted wire with sparkling beads and silky cord

You are going to learn lots of new techniques in this project and have lots of fun with it – twisting wire, using different types of beads, making knots and attaching cord fold-over ends.

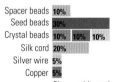

Spacer beads	**10%**		
Seed beads	**30%**		
Crystal beads	**10%**	**10%**	**10%**
Silk cord	**20%**		
Silver wire	**5%**		
Copper	**5%**		
Clasp and jump ring			

MATERIALS AND TOOLS

- 441 of size 11 matt metallic beads
- 10 of 4 mm Swarovski crystal bicone fireopal (gold) beads
- 7 of 6 mm Swarovski crystal bicone montana (blue) beads
- 7 of 6 mm Swarovski crystal bicone padparadscha (red) beads
- 1 of 7 mm round copper jump rings
- 2 of 5 mm oval copper jump rings
- 0.4 mm (26-gauge) silver wire
- 50 cm (20 in) of 3 mm gold silk cord
- 6 of 5 mm antique gold rings
- 2 of 6 mm copper cord fold-over ends
- 1 12 mm copper lobster clasp
- Chain-nose pliers
- Flat-nose pliers
- Wire cutters
- Ruler
- Scissors
- Thread Zapper

See also

Spacers and metal components, page 76
Other stringing materials, page 83

1 Thread all 441 matt metallic beads onto the wire. If your wire is still on a reel, push the beads up to the reel. If not, thread one bigger bead to the end of your wire and twist some wire beneath it. This will act as a 'stop' at the end.

2 Bring the first 21 matt metallic beads down the wire and shape them into a loop.

3 Twist the wire and continue twisting until you create a short stem.

4 Push another 21 matt metallic beads close to your existing loop, bend them into a loop and twist until you create another short stem.

5 Continue shaping 21 loops with 21 stems and shape them into the flower form. Remove the 'stop' bead or reel.

6 Thread on one red Swarovski bicone bead and make one loop a little bit bigger than the other loops. Push the bead into the middle of the loop.

7 Hold the red Swarovski bead and start twisting. Continue twisting until the wire is twisted all the way down to the centre of the flower and stays firmly in place.

8 Push the wire through the wired centre of your flower and make a loop a little bit bigger than the flower loops. Thread on the blue Swarovski bead and twist again, as in Step 7.

9 Continue threading on all red, blue, and gold Swarovski beads in this way. Once all of the beads are threaded on, secure your wire by twisting it a few times around the centre of the flower, and cut any remaining wire off with wire cutters.

10 Cut 50 cm (20 in) of 3 mm gold silk cord. Make a knot about 3 cm (1⅛ in) from the centre. Thread on six antique gold rings and make another knot at the end of the row of beads.

11 Thread the cord through the pendant and through one of the petals, so that the six rings are on one side. Now make a knot and add six more rings, followed by a knot on the other side.

12 Place one end of the silk cord into the copper cord fold-over end. Make sure that a loop of the cord end is facing away from the main necklace. Press one side of the copper end with flat-nose pliers, making sure that it holds the cord firmly in place.

13 Press the other side of the copper cord fold-over end with flat-nose pliers, so it is on top of the first one. Double check that the silk cord is securely attached.

14 If necessary, trim off the overlapping silk cord with sharp scissors or a Thread Zapper. Attach another copper cord end to the other side of the necklace.

15 Use the oval copper jump ring to attach the copper lobster clasp. Attach the oval copper jump ring, followed by the round copper jump ring on the other side of the necklace.

Handbag charm

Make a cheap handbag look more expensive

Chains can be used in many ways; they're not just for bracelets and necklaces. This fun project shows you another creative way to use chains in your work. You can wear this project on your handbag, on a belt or to personalize your keys.

MATERIALS AND TOOLS

- 9 of 10 mm acrylic silver ball charms
- 1 10 mm silver bead cap
- 60 cm (24 in) (or 88 links) of 5 mm silver double loop chain
- 1 35 mm silver lobster key ring
- 10 cm (4 in) of 1 mm (18-gauge) silver wire
- Wire cutters
- Needle file
- Chain-nose pliers
- Flat-nose pliers
- Round-nose pliers
- Crimping pliers
- Needle file

Bead note

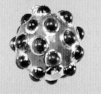

- Glass beads add texture and sparkle to your design, but also extra weight so bear that in mind when planning.

Variation:
Mix-and-match charms

Different types of charms and beads can be attached to the end of your chain links. Don't be afraid to mix and match your beads and charms.

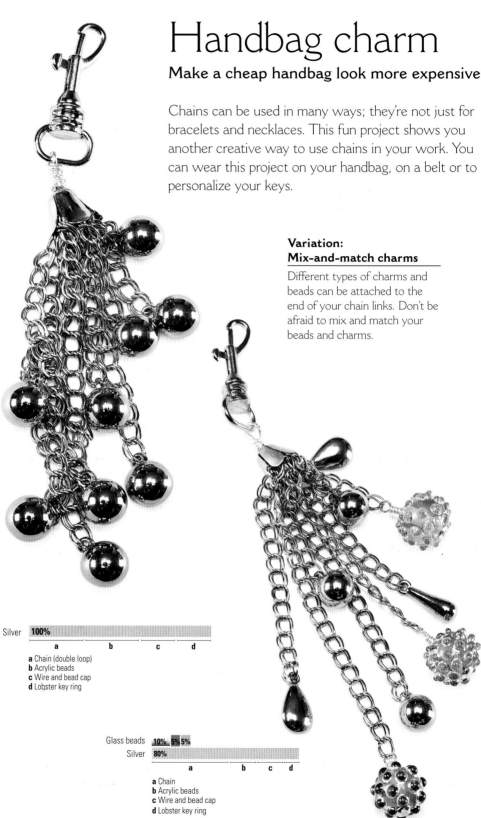

Silver	100%			
	a	b	c	d

a Chain (double loop)
b Acrylic beads
c Wire and bead cap
d Lobster key ring

Glass beads	10%	5%	5%	
Silver	80%			
	a	b	c	d

a Chain
b Acrylic beads
c Wire and bead cap
d Lobster key ring

See also
Plastic and acrylic beads, page 58
Chain and wire, page 79

1 Start to create the different lengths of chain. With the chain-nose pliers and flat-nose pliers, take hold of one side of the 20th link and carefully open that link.

2 Hold open the link with the chain-nose pliers and place the loop of one 10 mm acrylic silver ball charm onto the chain link. Close the link.

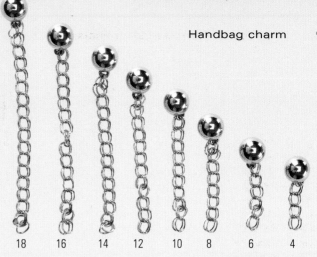

18 16 14 12 10 8 6 4

3 Repeat this process for the following chain lengths: 18 links, 16 links, 14 links, 12 links, 10 links, 8 links, 6 links and finally, 4 links.

4 Cut a 10 cm (4 in) length of 1 mm (18-gauge) wire. File one end of the wire. Place the filed end of the wire between the two jaws of your round-nose pliers. You are going to form a large loop. Move the wire almost to the end of your round-nose pliers and form the loop.

5 Place all the chain links onto the loop, starting with the longest one and finishing with the shortest one. Close the loop with the round-nose pliers. Make sure that the chain links are securely attached.

6 Put the bead cap on your wire and push the loop inside of the bead cap. This way you can hide all of the tops of the chains.

7 Using the round-nose pliers, form a loop on the top of your bead cap, but don't close your loop completely.

8 Add a silver lobster key ring inside the loop.

9 Wrap the wire around the main wire.

10 Cut any remaining wire off with wire cutters.

11 Use the top hole of your crimping pliers to push the end of the wire in.

Sieve-based brooch

Beautifully detailed freestyle project with a vintage look

'Vintage' has become fashionable again and wearing brooches is a style statement. Brooch sieves comes in different shapes and sizes, but the most common ones are a basic round or oval shape. Having more holes in your sieve will give you the flexibility to use different sizes of beads. Use double thread to attach your beads, as the sieve perforations may be quite sharp and can easily snap your thread. You could also use thin wire instead of thread – or a combination of the two.

Acrylic leaf	**10%**	**15%**	
Polymer clay rose	**10%**	**10%**	**10%**
Glass leaf	**10%**	**15%**	
Pearl beads	**20%**		

1 Cut approx 90 cm (1 yd) of nylon thread, thread it through your needle, and bring both ends of the thread next to each other. Tie them together in a knot. Place a dab of clear nail polish on top of your knot.

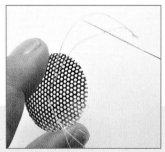

2 Secure the thread by going up through the centre hole of the sieve and returning through another hole (a couple of holes away). Then take the thread through the middle of the threads above your knot and give it a hard pull to ensure it is secure.

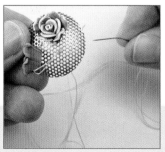

3 Bring the needle and thread out through the centre of the top of the sieve and attach the pink polymer clay rose. Go through the sieve and back through the bead again to strengthen it. Attach the brown polymer clay rose below the pink one, using the same technique.

4 Place the light pink polymer clay rose onto the sieve and place the leaves around your flowers. You might run out of thread. If so, be sure to make a knot at the end of your thread and put a little clear nail polish on your knot to help seal it. Then use the technique from Step 1 to attach a new length of thread. Continue attaching the leaf beads. Make sure that the beads do not feel too loose.

Bead note

• A polymer clay rose can bring an elegant look to your piece. Attach the rose using the hole through its base.

Acrylic leaf	10%	15%	
Polymer clay rose	10%	10%	10%
Glass leaf	15%		10%
Pearl beads	20%		

Brooch pins are easy to attach by folding their prongs over the sieve using pliers. They will cover your knots and threads and give a neat and professional finish.

Variation: Chop and change

Mix up different leaves, flower types or beads however you want, to make different brooches.

5 Once all of the leaves are attached, sew a few small light brown faux pearls onto the sieve.

6 When you have finished attaching the pearl beads, make a knot and put a little bit of clear nail polish on the top of the knot. Cut off any remaining thread.

7 Put some glue onto the back of the sieve and attach the brooch pin.

8 Bend all six tiny prongs over the sieve using chain-nose pliers. Make sure that the brooch pin is securely attached.

> ***See also***
> *Plastic and acrylic beads, page 58*
> *Spacers and metal components, page 76*

MATERIALS AND TOOLS

- 250 of 2.5 mm ivory faux pearls
- 5 of 4 mm ivory faux pearls
- 1 of 12 mm ivory faux pearls
- 5 of 4 mm crystal beads
- Silver tiara band
- 0.8 mm (20-gauge) silver wire
- 0.4 mm (26-gauge) silver wire
- Wire cutters
- Chain-nose pliers

Crystal flower tiara
Wire-twisting technique with crystals and pearls

Brides traditionally wear tiaras, but they can be easily customized to become an everyday accessory, not just for special occasions. Different types of tiara headbands are available – gold or silver, single or double, smooth or textured, with or without a comb and many more.

See also

Design styles, page 32
Crystal beads, page 60
Chain and wire, page 79

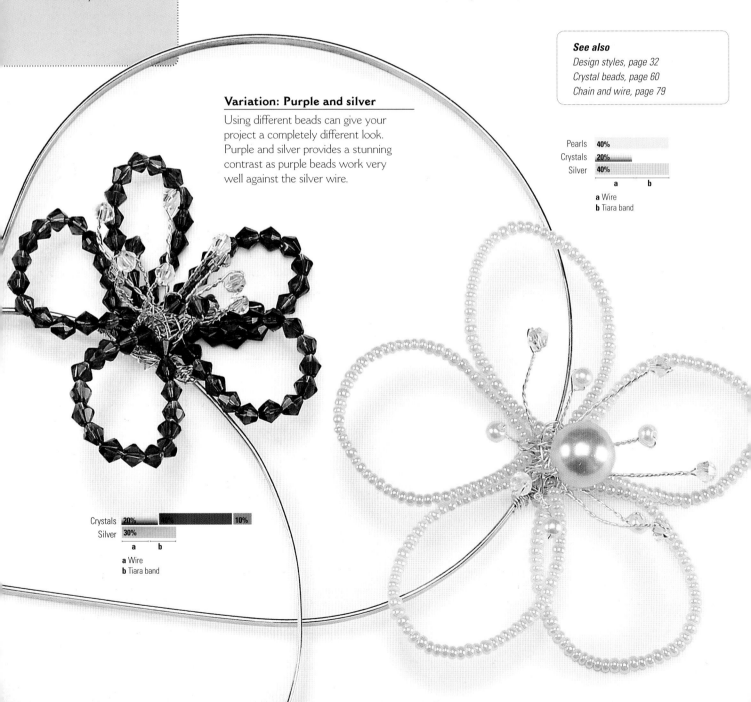

Variation: Purple and silver

Using different beads can give your project a completely different look. Purple and silver provides a stunning contrast as purple beads work very well against the silver wire.

Pearls **40%**
Crystals **20%**
Silver **40%**
     a   **b**
a Wire
b Tiara band

Crystals **20%**   **40%**   **10%**
Silver **30%**
  a   **b**
a Wire
b Tiara band

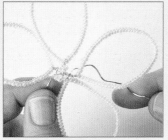

3 Cut 50 cm (20 in) of 0.4 mm (26-gauge) silver wire. Thread the crystal beads onto the wire. Bend the wire about 10 cm (4 in) from the end and bring one crystal bead into the centre of the bent wire. Hold the bead between your fingers and twist the bead until the wire is twisted tightly together, creating a stem about 3 cm (1⅛ in) long.

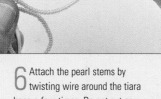

1 Thread 250 ivory 2.5 mm faux pearls onto the 0.8 mm (20-gauge) wire and push it close to the reel. Separate the 50 pearls closest to the end of wire and bend this beaded section into a loop. Twist the wire loop together at the base.

2 Continue making another five loops with 50 ivory faux pearls each time, to create a little flower. Attach the flower to the side of the tiara by twisting the wire around the tiara base. Cut off any remaining wire.

4 Now bend 4 cm (1⅝ in) of wire and thread on a 4 mm ivory faux pearl. Bring the pearl into the centre and twist it the same way as you did with the crystal bead.

5 Continue – making five pearl stems and five crystal bead stems.

6 Attach the pearl stems by twisting wire around the tiara base a few times. Do not cut any remaining wire just yet.

7 Attach the crystal stems in the middle of the pearl flower, by twisting wire around the tiara base and centre of the pearl stems a few times. Do not cut any remaining wire just yet.

8 Thread both ends of the wire through each side of the 12 mm ivory faux pearl and attach firmly in the middle of the flower.

9 Secure the wire by wrapping the excess around the tiara base several times.

10 Cut off the remaining wire if necessary. Use chain-nose pliers to flatten the wire to the band.

11 Use your fingers to gently form nice loops for the petals on your flower. Finally, bend each pearl and crystal strand, facing up and away from the flower loops.

MATERIALS AND TOOLS

- 50 mm cherry quartz doughnut pendant
- 8 of 16 mm sponge (pressed) round coral beads
- 6 of 15 mm coral rondelle beads
- 2 of 30 mm antique silver beads
- 23 of 2 mm smooth silver ball beads
- 4 of 7 mm antique silver spacer rings
- 4 of 10 mm antique silver flower bead caps
- 18 of 7 mm hard silver oval jump rings
- 35 mm silver doughnut holder
- 127cm (50 in) of 1 mm (18-gauge) silver wire
- Silver hook clasp
- Wire cutters
- Chain-nose pliers
- Flat-nose pliers
- Round-nose pliers
- Crimping pliers
- Needle file
- Ruler

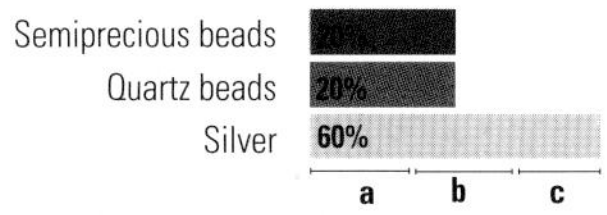

Semiprecious beads
Quartz beads   20%
Silver   60%

a   b   c

a Wire
b Bead spacers and bead caps
c Doughnut holder and clasp

Wire-wrapped bead necklace

Beautiful and intricate beading technique with endless possibilities

Practise this wire wrapping technique on square beads first, because they are much easier to work with. The rounds will be more of a challenge. Using different thicknesses of wire will give very different results. Heavier wires hold their shape better. In this project, 1 mm (18-gauge) wire is used for coiling around the beads. For added interest, smaller beads can be strung onto your wire and wrapped around the beads along the length of wire.

Semiprecious beads	**40%**	
Antique silver	**20%**	
Silver	**40%**	

a   b   c

a Wire
b Bead caps
c Clasp

Variation: Colour change

For a different look, use a different doughnut holder finding, a turquoise pendant and turquoise beads.

> ### See also
> *Semiprecious beads, page 48*
> *Spacers and metal components, page 76*
> *Chain and wire, page 79*

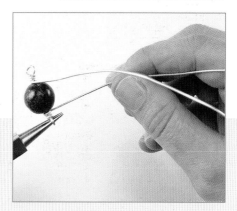

1   Cut 30 cm (12 in) of 1 mm (18-gauge) silver wire, using the wire cutters. File both ends of the wire flat, using a needle file. Thread on one 16 mm round coral bead, and place it in the middle of the wire. Then bend up the wire approx 5 mm (³⁄₁₆ in) from the bead hole on each side of the bead.

2   Create a loop on each side of the bead, leaving a 5 mm (³⁄₁₆ in) gap between each loop and the bead. Use round-nose pliers to do this.

3   Hold the loop with flat-nose pliers and wrap the wire tightly around the wire about three times, beneath the loop, to form small circles. Do not cut off any remaining wire. Use crimping pliers to neatly squeeze the wrapping if necessary.

4 Keep wrapping the wire around the bead, until you create three wire coils sitting neatly on the top of your bead. Using the same technique, repeat this on other side of the bead. Do not cut off any remaining wire.

5 Wrap one wire across the bead so that it goes diagonally down towards the other coil. Now take the other wire, and wrap it so that it goes diagonally up in the other direction along the bottom of the other wire.

6 Grasp the end of one wire with round-nose pliers and start to coil it back towards the bead. Stop when you have made a small coil. Grasp the end of the second wire and create a small coil using the same technique.

10 Cut 5 cm (2 in) of wire for the next link and thread on one 2 mm silver ball bead, followed by a 30 mm antique silver bead, followed by another 2 mm silver ball bead. Make a single loop on each side of the beads, using round-nose pliers. Repeat these steps again to create a second identical link.

11 Next, make a pendant hook. Cut 11 cm (4⅜ in) of wire. File both sides of the wire flat. Thread on 15 of the 2 mm silver ball beads and place them in the middle of the wire. Bend the wire around a metal bar (or similar object), keeping the beads in the middle.

12 Make a loop on both sides of the wire, using round-nose pliers. Hold one of your loops with flat-nose pliers and keep coiling until you come close to your beads. Do not complete a second coil yet.

16 Use another 7 mm hard silver oval jump ring to attach the antique silver bead links onto your three beaded links.

17 Next, attach four wire-wrapped beads on both sides (one by one), using 7 mm hard silver oval jump rings.

18 Finally, attach three jump rings followed by a clasp hook-and-eye on each side of the necklace.

7 Using your finger, push both small coils closer to the bead, so they sit neatly. Repeat Steps 1 to 7 to create another seven wire-wrapped bead links (eight in total).

8 Cut 10 cm (4 in) of wire for the other link. Thread on the beads in the order shown. Bend the wire up at each end of the beads, leaving a 5 mm (³⁄₁₆ in) gap on each side.

9 Make a loop, then wrap the wire around itself – do this on both sides. Make one more link, repeating Steps 8 and 9.

13 Push the uncoiled end of the hook through the 35 mm silver doughnut holder, keeping the beads and doughnut in the middle of the hook. Complete coiling on the other side of the hook.

14 Attach a 50 mm cherry quartz doughnut pendant onto the silver doughnut holder.

15 Use 7 mm hard silver oval jump rings to attach the three beaded links onto each side of the hook.

Sara Cohen's bracelets are made using silver mesh combined with freshwater pearls (above) and sugar beads (below).

Resources

Suppliers

Beads Direct
www.beadsdirect.co.uk
0870 086 9877

Bead Scene, The
PO Box 6351
Towcester, Northamptonshire
NN12 7YX
01327 353639
www.thebeadscene.com

Bead Shop, The
21a Tower Street
Covent Garden
London WC2H 9NS
0207 240 0931
www.beads.co.uk

Beads Unlimited
PO Box 1
Hove
Sussex BN3 3SG
01273 740777
www.beadsunlimited.co.uk

Beadworks
The Bead Shop
21a Tower Street
London WC2
020 8553 3240
www.beadworks.co.uk

Creative Beadcraft
20 Beak Street
London W1
020 7629 9964
www.creativebeadcraft.co.uk

Exchange Findings
11–13 Hatton Wall
London EC1N 8HX
020 7831 7574
www.cooksongold.com

International Craft
Unit 4, The Empire Centre
Imperial Way
Watford, WD24 4YH
01923 235 336
www.internationalcraft.com

London Bead Co, The
339 Kentish Town Rd
London NW5 2TJ
0870 203 2323
www.londonbeadco.co.uk

Pandorion
www.pandorion.co.uk
01206 868623

Scientific Wire Company, The
www.wires.co.uk
020 8505 0002

Spellbound Bead Company, The
www.spellbound.co.uk
01543 417650

Stitch 'n' Craft
www.stitchncraft.co.uk
01747 830666

Online resources

abeadstore.com
A selection of simple beading projects, tips, FAQs and a retail area.

www.auntiesbeads.com
Online retailer with a wide range of beads and findings as well as resources for weekly projects and video tutorials.

www.beadersshowcase.com
An online community with a place to showcase your work and chat to other members.

www.beadingdaily.com
Site containing projects, information, contests, galleries and chat.

www.beadingtimes.com
Excellent source of information on all aspects of jewellery design. Updated monthly.

www.beadmagazine.co.uk
Site with projects, galleries and forums. Also Bead TV, showing tutorials, workshops and demonstrations.

www.beadwork.about.com
A site with an active forum and a lot of links and articles.

www.beadworkersguild. org.uk
A membership site publishing a journal and a selection of books, as well as running workshops and beading events.

www.crystalgems.co.uk
Information regarding crystal and gemstone properties and how they can be used with chakras and as remedies.

www.enijewelry.com
Amazing online tutorials on wire work; pay to download the projects you require or follow free links to beginners' lessons.

www.firemountain.com
Online retailer with a huge range of gemstones and other supplies as well as an 'encycloBEADia', gallery and tutorials section.

www.jewelinfo4u.com
A vast source of information ranging from gemstone data to tools required for jewellery making and designer galleries.

www.merchantsoverseas.com
Information on all things Swarovski, with colour, shape and size charts, seasonal colour trends and an online retail area.

www.wire-sculpture.com
Excellent resource centre on wire and metal skills, containing projects and ideas as well as information on pricing and marketing your work.

Magazines

Bead Magazine
www.beadmagazine.co.uk

Beadstyle
www.beadstylemag.com
Bi-monthly magazine with tutorials and supply lists incorporating a wide range of materials.

Bead and Button
www.beadandbutton.com
A magazine packed with loads of projects to challenge and inspire readers of all interests and abilities.

Table of common seed beads

This table shows the vital statistics of a number of common bead sizes. This will give you an idea of the physical size of each of the bead sizes and the amount of beads per gram.

	Seed bead size	Beads per 2.5 cm (inch)	Approximate size	Number per 1 gram	Number per 10 grams	Number per 100 grams
	Size 15	24	1.5 mm	250	2,500	25,000
	Size 11	18	2.2 mm	120	1,200	12,000
	Size 8	13	3 mm	36	360	3,600
	Size 6	10	3.7 mm	18	180	1,800
	Cylinder bead size	Beads per 2.5 cm (inch)	Approximate size	Number per 1 gram	Number per 10 grams	Number per 100 grams
	Size 15	19	1.3 mm	290	2,900	29,000
	Size 11	20	1.6 mm	200	2,000	20,000

Wire gauge

Wire is either sold in millimetres (mm) or by gauge (ga), both of which refer to its diameter. The gauge commonly used is American Wire Gauge (AWG). Although these don't match up exactly, a rough conversion is usually close enough for most wirework.

mm	AWG
0.1	38
0.15	34
0.2	32
0.25	30
0.3	28
0.4	26
0.5	24
0.6	22
0.7	21
0.8	20
0.9	19
1	18
1.2	16
1.5	14
2	12

Hard or soft?

Wire is sold in different levels of hardness: soft; hard; and half-hard, each of which has its ideal uses.

Hardness	Ideal for	Unsuitable for
Soft	Wrapping around another wire – it won't harden and become brittle as you work it.	Making clasps or components – it will be too soft to have the strength you need.
Hard	Making clasps and weight-bearing components – it has the strength to keep its shape.	Wrapping or any techniques that requires a lot of work – the wire will become very difficult to manipulate and too hard on your hands.
Half-hard	All types of wirework – it is versatile. Don't choose half-hard if you need a really soft or hard wire, but otherwise it is an ideal substitute.	

Common bead shapes

Not all beads are round. They come in many shapes and sizes. Below are some of the most common with their names and how their holes lie:

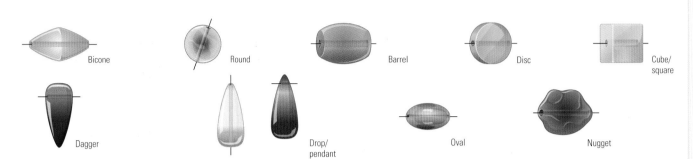

Bicone   Round   Barrel   Disc   Cube/square

Dagger   Drop/pendant   Oval   Nugget

Estimating quantities

You'll find that the size of beads varies according to manufacturer, finish on the bead and even colour of the bead. This table shows an approximation of the average sizes and quantities.

	Bead (approximate size)	Beads per 2.5 cm (1 in)	Beads per 46 cm (18 in)	Beads per 61 cm (24 in)
	Size 15 seed bead (1.5 mm)	17	307	401
	Size 11 seed bead (1.8–2.2 mm)	12–14	210–256	278–339
	Size 8 seed bead (3.3 mm)	8	140	185
	Size 6 seed bead (4 mm)	6	115	153
	2 mm bead	12	230	305
	3 mm bead	8	154	203
	4 mm bead	6	115	153
	5 mm bead	5	92	122
	6 mm bead	4	77	102
	8 mm bead	3	57	76
	10 mm bead	2	46	61
	12 mm bead	2	38	51
	13 mm bead	2	35	47

	Bead (approximate size)	Beads per 2.5 cm (1 in)	Beads per 46 cm (18 in)	Beads per 61 cm (24 in)
	14 mm bead	1-2	33	43
	15 mm bead	1	30	40
	16 mm bead	1	29	38
	17 mm bead	1	27	36
	18 mm bead	1	25	34
	20 mm bead	1	23	30

Glossary

AWG
American Wire Gauge. The measurement used to sell wire in the USA.

Back through
To thread back through a bead in the opposite direction.

Bead reamer
Tool used to enlarge or smooth bead holes.

Bead soup
A mix of beads in different shapes, sizes and colours.

Bugle bead
Long, tubular seed bead.

Calottes
Small findings, also called clamshells, necklace tips or knot cups, used to hide unsightly knots in thread or to fasten the stringing material to the clasp.

Chain-nose pliers
Pliers with flat inner jaws that taper to a point. Also called snipe-nose pliers.

Cloisonné bead
Patterned bead made of filigree metal coloured with enamel glazes.

Crimp beads
Small metal beads that, when squashed with crimping pliers, bite into the nylon surface of flexible beading wire to secure.

Crimping
The act of squashing crimp beads to secure them onto flexible beading wire.

Crimping pliers
Pliers with two specially designed notches used to squash crimp beads.

Eyepin
A length of wire with a loop at one end.

Findings
The small metal pieces used to finish jewellery, such as clasps, crimps or earring hooks.

Flat-nose pliers
Pliers with a flat inner jaw, the same width all the way along.

Flexible beading wire
A series of very fine strands of stainless steel coated in nylon, used to string jewellery and to finish with crimp beads. Also called beading or stringing wire, or beading cable.

Gauge (ga)
A term used to indicate the thickness of wire.

Gimp
Also called French wire, this is used to protect your thread from rubbing against metal findings.

Headpin
A length of wire with a wider end that stops beads from falling off.

Hex-cut bead
Bead with hexagonal sides.

Jump ring
Small loop of metal that can be used to attach findings.

Lampwork
A technique for making handmade glass beads using rods of glass heated in a flame and moulded over a metal mandrel.

Mandrel
A metal rod used to form jump rings or glass beads.

Rosary pliers
Round-nose pliers with wire cutters in the handles specially designed to make rosary (or turned) loops.

Round-nose pliers
Pliers with rounded jaws that taper to a point.

Skip a bead
Missing a bead and threading through the next one.

Split ring
These are used to attach findings to your jewellery.

Stop bead
Also called a tension bead. A bead added to the start of your work to stop other beads from falling off the thread, and to help you maintain tension.

Tail-thread
The end of thread that you leave at the start and end of your work to use later to finish your beadwork.

Tension
How tight or loose your finished beadwork is.

Turned loop
A small loop at the end of a wire. Also known as a rosary loop.

Wrapped loop
A decorative and secure method of creating a loop on wire.

Many bead shapes can be incorporated into one piece: here, bicones, cubes, ovals, faceted rounds and more.

Index

Sue Edwards' necklace is made with turquoise tiger tail wire, turquoise and matching beads, silver wire 'dangles' and a coloured shell pendant.

Credits

Quarto would like to thank the following artists for supplying beaded pieces:

Aliki Stroumpouli, www.alikistroumpouli.com – *pages 8, 14c*
Alisha Leow, www.bohemianbutterfly1.etsy.com – *page 17*
Carol Blackburn, carolblackburn.co.uk – *pages 2, 11br, 14bl*
Chris & Joy Poupazis, www.cjpoupazis.com – *pages 14tr, 16bl/r, 20t, 23tr*
Deborah Millsop, www.deborahclairemillsop.blogspot.com – *pages 21cr, 25l, 34b*
Karin Chilton, www.siriusjewellery.co.uk – *pages 9l/c, 21tr, 22cl/bl, 25ctr*
Kim Gover, www.bead-e-licious.co.uk – *pages 5t, 15tr, 31tl/tr (inner piece)*
Margaret Bonham, www.vtcrafts.net, www.facebook.com/mags.bonham –
page 30bl
Moira Clinch – *page 13tr*
Nicole Stanley, www.hollybirdbeads.co.uk – *pages 12cl, 24t*
Penny Akester, www.pitstopx.co.uk – *pages 4, 13tl, 23br, 24br*
Purvi Sanghvi, www.purvisanghvi.com – *pages 12b, 31t (outer piece)*
Sara Cohen – *page 136*
Sue Edwards, www.sueedwardsjewellery.co.uk – *page 143*
Vintage – *pages 13c, 27b, 30br*

All other images are the copyright of Quarto Publishing plc. While every effort has been made to credit contributors, Quarto would like to apologize should there have been any omissions or errors – and would be pleased to make the appropriate correction for future editions of the book.

Quarto would also like to thank the following suppliers:

Rainbow Colour Selector, K1C2, LLC, www.k1c2.com—*pages 10, 12*
Spellbound Bead Co © www.spellboundbead.co.uk – *pages 38t, p39t/c/cl*
The Potomac Bead Company ® www.potomacbeads.com – *page 39cr*

Author dedication
To to my lovely husband, Simon Graham, thank you for your patience and help. To Nicky Watson for the use of her wonderful Long Chain Necklace project. To Christine Graham and Nathan Yansifski for their help proofreading and for making me laugh. To the very supportive and helpful Quarto team who discovered me and made all this happen.